CATALOGUE OF SHORTER & SON

TOBY AND CHARACTER JUGS

1917-1970

by
Bernard McDonald

ACKNOWLEDGEMENTS

This is the most enjoyable part of the book I have written, not just because its the last page, but it gives me the opportunity to thank the people who have helped put this book together, and most important the new friends I have made.

Special thanks for advice to Steve Mullins friend and Toby Jug expert USA, Eddie Templeman Toby Jug expert UK, and now a valued friend.

Thanks Eddie for getting me started on the book and all your helpful advice.

Special thanks for supplying photographs, without their help it would have been impossible to complete.

Steve Mullins and David Fastenau, authors of *Toby and Character Jugs of the 20th Century and their Makers*.

For their help, Irene and Gordon Hopwood, authors of *The Shorter Connection*, Geoffrey Godden author of *Encyclopaedia of British Pottery and Porcelain Marks*, Mary Gilhooly archivist for The D'Oyly Carte Opera Company, Phil Martin archivist at Companies House, London.

Jon Blade and all the staff at Flaydemouse.

To collectors Darrell Edwards and Adam Gywnne.

Last but not least, four lovely people, Jan and Robin Cross. Anne and Ken Jones who invited myself and my wife to stay at their beautiful homes, to view and photograph part of their amazing Shorter collections.

Print, design and reproduction by Flaydemouse, Yeovil, Somerset
Published by Bernard McDonald
© 2002 Bernard McDonald
ISBN 0 9544086 0 8
British Library Cataloguing-in-Publication Data. A catalogue record for this book is available from the British Library

DEDICATIONS

To my lovely wife Mary, for all you had to put up with while I was putting this book together. For your support and understanding when things were going wrong and giving me the strength to carry on.
Love you.

To the passing of the late and great, the king of Toby Jug collectors, Vic Schuler, who inspired us all. You will always be with us.
God bless you.

INTRODUCTION

The idea for this book came about by conversing with collectors of Shorter Toby Jugs, discussing the different colourway and sizes of the jugs. I decided then that what we need is more information than is available at present available on Shorter Toby and Character Jugs. I acknowledge the phenomenal work done by Steve Mullins and David Fastenau in their book *Toby and Character Jugs of the 20th Century and their Makers.* By producing a book on world Tobies and Character Jugs I realise that they could not take a much closer look at every individual pottery and all the different characteristics that go with all the different colourways, sizes, and unrecorded jugs etc, etc. If your Toby collecting includes jugs from other potteries, then this book by Steve Mullins and David Fastenau is a must for you. It includes information and illustrations from 150 potteries worldwide. We would like to take this opportunity to acknowledge also the great work of Irene and Gordon Hopwood in their book *The Shorter Connection,* an excellent history on the Shorter family and its factories. If you collect the wonderful items of flatware from the three Shorter factories, ie, Shorter, Wilkinson and Newport, I strongly recommend you read or obtain a copy of this book by Irene and Gordon Hopwood. Steve Mullins, David Fastenau, Irene and Gordon Hopwood have pioneered the way forwards for the Shorter collectors, its up to the rest of us to push the boundaries even farther, and complete the Shorter collection. I asked collectors what would we as collectors like to see in a book on Shorter Toby and Character Jugs (1), we would like to see a really good close-up of every Toby (2) all the information about the Toby including the price guide laid out on the same page as the illustration (3) the Genuine Shorter backstamps that were used on the Toby and Character Jugs. To us, this would make it a lot easier to understand, but then came the problems of trying to find out what Shorter and Son Ltd Toby and Character Jugs were produced and where could I find all these jugs to photograph for the book. The first problem, trying to obtain information on Shorter Toby Jugs was almost impossible, Irene and Gordon Hopwood were very helpful, but admit there is very little information available on Shorter Toby and Character Jugs. A lot of information in this book has been with the help of collectors from many different parts of the world. I must give a special mention to Eddie Templeman a real expert on Shorter Toby Jugs for spending hours of his time on the telephone helping me with information needed to complete this book. Second problem where to find all the jugs to photograph for the book. Some of the Shorter Toby and Character Jugs are so rare and do not often come on the market for sale, this was a major headache. Then came the offer of help from two of the most generous people it has been my good fortune to know. Steve Mullins and David Fastenau authors of *Toby and Character Jugs of the 20th Century and their Makers* they agreed to forward all the photographs they had taken and used in their own book. Without this help from these two giants of the Toby world this book would have been almost impossible to complete. Thanks guys we and all Shorter Toby collectors are in your debt for this splendid gesture. The last and biggest problem. With the time lapse of the closure of the Shorter Factory at Copeland Street, Stoke-on-Trent in 1964, and Shorter moving in to the Crown Devon Factory with a small workforce in 1964-1970, to present day, was the date as to when Shorter became a Limited Company, I had the date 1933 from Irene and Gordon Hopwood in their book *The Shorter Connection*, 1933 from Steve Mullins and David Fastenau Book *Toby and Character Jugs of the 20th Century.* Geoffrey Godden author of *Encyclopaedia of British Pottery and Porcelain Marks* kindly offered to help with this date, Geoffrey's answer was also 1933. I also checked with Companies House in London, even though they informed me all the Shorter records had been destroyed, they were certain that there was no record of Shorter being a limited company before 1933. Why should this be a problem you might ask, every Shorter Toby and Character Jug I have seen or know of number over one thousand, all have 'Ltd' in the backstamp, so you can see why the date Shorter was declared a limited company was so important to me. This still left the question what Toby and Character Jugs were produced from 1917 to 1933. Some of the jugs referred to by the *Pottery Gazette* are 9" female Toby cloaked with her hair in a bun under a Tricorn hat, clasping a jug of ale with both hands. I know about the other jugs referred to, the Hollins Toby, the Coachman etc because they were re-issued after 1933 by Shorter and have 'Ltd' in the backstamp, but I am still left with the unsolved what came before 1933, were these jugs marked Shorter, were they backstamped at all. Then! Bingo! They say everything comes to those who wait. Listed on Ebay was a S/S Toby that looked familiar, but there was something different about it. I could not quite work out what it was so I emailed the seller to ask for a photograph of the backstamp which was not shown in the listing. The seller responded very quickly to my request, then as I scrolled the photograph there was the answer to my quest, Shorter & Son, Stoke-on-Trent, England. I now have the Toby in my possession (see *Toby*) and the evidence I needed to show you what backstamp Shorter used on their pre 1933 Toby and Character Jugs.

COLLECTING SHORTER TOBIES

Why collect Shorter Toby and Character Jugs you might ask. The Shorter Toby collection, over 240 items in all, offers some of the most fascinating items on the market today. Some of the early jugs are not far off the magic antique rating of 100 years old. This being the case, they are starting to be a really good investment as well as the excitement of putting your collection together. You will see by the listings in the book there is something for everyone to collect. Some of the Shorter items already command very high prices on the auctions and with antique dealers, and I think they will carry on increasing at a steady rate, such is the interest in the Shorter Jugs at present. When speaking to Steve Mullins about Shorter Tobies, he always comments 'It's ugly enough to be a Shorter Toby' which always makes me smile, but I understand what he means. Shorter Tobies have that something special about them that you do not get from other potteries. About the jugs, some of the later jugs are very scarce and hard to find, speaking to Eddie Templeman and Steve Mullins about this we are of the opinion, and this is

only theory, the shortage of the later issues could be due to the fact, they were being produced in the late 1963-1964, then unbeknown to Shorter, looming over them was the closure of this famous factory. If this was the case, there is the reason why some of the later jugs are very scarce, production of them ceased with the closure of the factory. Also when you start your collection you will find a number of the jugs unnamed, these are Shorter's early models from 1917-1933. The jugs not being named has caused a lot of confusion as to their correct name. Lionel Bailey who at one time owned about a third of the Shorter moulds, and also had probably one of the finest collections of Shorter Toby and Character Jugs, tells me it was just a case of people not knowing who these characters were, so they just called them by what seemed an apt name. This could have been the case with the *Mr* and *Mrs Farmer*. It was my aim to try and show you an illustration of every Shorter Jug, but alas one has escaped the net the *Butlers* Character Jug, if I can obtain a photograph of this jug, or any unrecorded jug that comes to light I will post them on the web site I have set up as a back up for further information. The L/S, M/S, S/S, refers to the size of the jugs ie; large, medium, and small size. due to the exchange rate changing daily, it was kept at $1.45 to £1 sterling ie; £10.00 = $14.50. For the purpose of the price guide in this book. the following unrecorded jugs were referred to in the Shorter records, but as of yet have not been verified as to were they ever issued or not.

UNRECORDED SHORTER JUGS

Abraham Lincoln	*Mrs Farmer*
Admiral	*Mr Punch*
George Washington	*Red Indian*
Guy of Gisborne	*Santa Claus*
Innkeeper	*Sheriff of Nottingham*
King of Hearts	*Sir Walter Scott*

If any collector has information on these unrecorded jugs, could you please contact me.
email address: bernie@shamrock59.freeserve.co.uk
web site address: http://mysite.freeserve.com/shorter

INTERNET

This is the best thing that has happened for the collector since collecting began. It would take two lifetimes of going to auctions and antique fairs everyday to try and find your Shorter wants, but now you can sit at home in comfort and view between 500 and 700 Toby and Character Jugs on any one day from the four corners of the planet going for auction. Ebay Auctions as far as I am concerned are the no 1 in the world, they are the best and make every part of buying and selling so easy even for the newcomer. A word of caution, you have in most cases one week to make your mind up about bidding for an item, so unless you are sure you are going to pay for the item do not bid on it, remember once you have bid you are liable to pay for the item. If you do not pay its not fair to the seller and will land you in hot water with Ebay. If you are unsure email the seller ask them about the item they are selling, what will the shipping cost be, are you liable for customs duty if its a costly item, how would they accept payment, you will find the sellers very helpful on Ebay. Foreign currency transactions were a nightmare until Paypal went international, like Ebay they have made buying and selling so easy in foreign currency dealings. You can pay for your items in minutes with a credit card, cuts out all the bank charges for international cheques, saves time on using the snail mail, and the Paypal charges are very low for the service they offer. Another point worth a mention never be put off by the shipping cost, just think if you had to get up on a winters morning travel a hundred miles to a decent antiques fair, hoping you might find that elusive jug, it makes the shipping cost seem very little in comparison. A word of advice for the overseas sellers. Most of Shorter's production of Toby and Character Jugs where exported to America, Canada, Australia, and New Zealand. Most of the Shorter collectors are in England, so why put an iron curtain up around your own country you see items listed on Ebay for instance, 'will ship to the USA only'. I know you don't realise but you have been giving the Tobies away for peanuts. this actually happened to me. A seller from the USA listed three Toby Jugs for sale, one of them was a Shorter *Pearly King*, I offered to bid $100 on his auction, and if I won he could keep the other two Toby Jugs to re-sell, as I only wanted the Shorter *Pearly King*. He refused to ship to the UK, the end result was the three Toby Jugs sold for $49 so come on you overseas sellers, take down the iron curtain and make yourself some real dollars, and help the Shorter collectors get the items they want.

BACKSTAMPS

Backstamps are the most important aid to collecting Shorter Tobies. There are so many copies of Shorter mugs and jugs around that you need to make sure your hard earned cash is being spent on the genuine article. Most of the well known Shorter backstamps are well documented and are easy to recognise, but watch out for the export backstamps where the name 'Shorter' is not included. For example, I saw a medium sized *Beefeater* Toby Jug for sale which I bought, which does not have the Shorter name included in the backstamp, but I knew it to be a Shorter Jug, because it is impressed 'Beefeater M/S', and 'Made in Great Britain' in black lettering. Now if this had been on a jug I did not recognise ie; one of the twelve listed in Steve Mullins and David Fastenau book *Toby and Character Jugs of the 20th Century and their Makers*, as jugs referred to in the Shorter records but not yet confirmed, you could easily miss turning up a real gem of a find. You will see listed the Genuine Shorter backstamps that are known, plus all the later copy backstamps to watch out for. Having said this, you might have to settle for a jug which is a copy from the same mould, because of the rarity of the piece if you want to complete your collection.

GENUINE BACKSTAMPS

You might find one or two backstamps worded slightly different than the following, but most of the known backstamps on the Toby Jugs are as follows. Owing to the poor quality of the Shorter backstamp and ink stamp I have decided it would be much better to print the text that appears on the backstamp. The following backstamps are in black ink.

Genuine Staffordshire Hand. Painted Shorter & Sons Ltd England	Includes	Shorter England Impressed or raised Model Name and Size
Genuine Staffordshire Hand Painted Shorter & Sons Ltd England	Without	Shorter England Impressed or raised Model Name and Size
Old Staffs Toby Shorter & Son Ltd Staffordshire Made in England	Includes	Shorter England Impressed With or Without Model Name and Size
Made in Great Britain	with only	Model Name and Size
Made in Great Britain	Includes	Shorter England Impressed with Model Name and Size
Genuine Staffordshire Made in England Shorter & Sons Ltd	Includes	Shorter England Impressed with Model Name and Size
Genuine Old Staffordshire Shorter England	Includes	Model Number Impressed
Shorter & Son Ltd Staffordshire Made in England	Without	Shorter England Impressed
Shorter & Son Ltd Stoke-on-Trent Made in Great Britain	Includes	Shorter England Impressed
Shorter & Son Ltd Stoke on Trent England	Without	Shorter England Impressed

The last backstamp above has also been seen in green ink on many export items to Australia but be careful with this one it is used a lot by the reproduction people.

The backstamp shown below is Shorter's pre-1933 stamp found on Toby and Character Jugs. Note you may also find this stamp with the word 'Sons', but as of yet it has not been recorded.

Shorter & Son Stoke-on-Trent England	Without	Shorter England Impressed

This unusual backstamp shown below was found on a circus type dog jug.

Purchased At Dickens Old Curiosity Shop London	With	Shorter England Impressed

GREEN BACKSTAMPS

This is quite a startling revelation you are about to read. The problem of identifying who did the green backstamps ie; (Genuine, Staffordshire, Hand Painted Shorter & Son Ltd, England) and dating them has caused me to lose sleep over this. It all starts with the closure of Shorter's in 1964, if you read the *Shorter Connection* by Irene and Gordon Hopwood that Shorter decided to merge with Crown Devon, and read other books on Crown Devon, that Crown Devon took over Shorter. The answer to the problem hangs on the two words merger or took over. Irene Hopwood tells me that a small workforce from the Shorter factory moved in with Crown Devon and had their own little corner of the factory to work in. It was never made clear as to what the actual arrangement was between Crown Devon and Shorter, but the main point being that Shorter were still Shorter making their own wares. Then comes the $64,000 dollar question who was responsible for the green backstamp on the Shorter Toby and Character Jugs between 1964-1970. The only answer is Shorter and not Crown Devon as stated in previous books. How did I come to this conclusion, between 1964-1970 John Shorter was still in control of Shorter, but in 1970 decided to opt out and retire from the pottery business, and he and his wife bought a post office in a country village. From the date that John retired you see the complete take over of Shorter by Crown Devon and the introduction of the Crown Devon backstamp on the Shorter Toby and Character Jugs along with the Shorter name. So from 1964-1970 the green backstamp is down to Shorter, why they decided to change from the black ink to green ink stamp, ie Genuine, Staffordshire, Hand Painted, Shorter & Son Ltd, England, I do not think we will ever know. But one of the main differences you will see from this time period 1964-1970 is the decline in the quality of the Toby and Character Jugs. We will mention two as an example first the *Scottie*, the tartan has been dropped from the paintwork, also inside his hat was formerly painted black, this is now in white glaze, the same with *Henry VIII*, lots of the paint work has been dropped, this was originally a beautiful jug full of colour, but now its a real poor quality Toby Jug. The reasons for the sudden change in quality was probably due to cost and staffing problems losing most of their experienced workers brought on by the move to the Crown Devon factory. Another big part of the green backstamp problem was the jugs finished in a honeyglaze and a dark green backstamp. In this honeyglaze finish you will also find many jugs with the black Shorter backstamp. I am 99% sure these jugs were made at the Wilkinson factory before Clarice Cliff sold it along with the Newport factory to Midwinter. the reason behind this thinking is I don't believe they were done by Crown Devon because some of the jugs I have in my possession with the honeyglaze finish were never reproduced by Crown Devon, ie; *Mr Farmer*, the *Fisherman*, the large *Beefeater* Character Gin Jug, and the *Parakeet* to name a few. Other evidence that points to Wilkinson's is I have items of flatware with the Wilkinson backstamp with the same honeyglaze finish as the Toby Jugs, also it is a well known glaze from this famous factory. A further clue is speaking to collectors whose families had bought some of the honeyglaze jugs with the dark green backstamp in the 1950s early 1960s and are still in their collections today. Why they would be produced from this factory is not known, there are lots of theories you can put forward, they were sub-contracted for some business reason, or Shorter could not handle their work load, let's not forget that even though the three factories operated under their own names, Wilkinson, Newport, and Shorter, they were all owned by Shorter, and we know the painters and modellers worked between the three factories ie; Clarice Cliff, Betty Silvester with their D'Oyly Carte designs, its not beyond the realms of possibility that the wares were made between the three factories. So to sum up all green backstamp Toby and Character jugs were made by Shorter even though the quality is not as good as in their hayday, but I must add the darker green stamp on the honeyglaze jugs are of good quality the only difference being they are of the modern production method ie; on the body parts the jugs have been air-brushed as opposed to hand painting, the rest of the jug is the same all hand painted. Would you believe as I am writing this, three *Father Neptune*'s have been listed on Ebay auctions, the first a L/S with the Genuine Backstamp in black ink, the second a L/S which has the dark green backstamp, and in the honeyglaze finish, is identical in its paintwork, except for the body parts as I have just mentioned being air-brushed, the third a M/S jug with the lighter green backstamp on the white glaze base. the paintwork on the latter is excellent, the only difference again the body parts being air-brushed. I would advise when purchasing Shorter Tobies for your collection and you come across the hard to find jug and its only available with the green backstamp on the white glaze jugs for example a *Mr Farmer* or *Mountaineer* they are worth buying at a good price because of their rarity, but if its a more common jug as the *Beefeater* or *Chelsea Pensioner* that the price would be less than that of the early jug with the black backstamp. Another backup to the honeyglaze green backstamp is you will see a lot of early pottery ie; Shantee tableware done in the honeyglaze with a black backstamp, maybe the green backstamp was used for costing between the two factories. it is also mentioned that Shorter and Wilkinson often shared the same stand at trade shows. So if you have bought a Shorter toby with a dark green backstamp on a honeyglaze finish its probably dated 1950s early 1960s. If it's a lighter green backstamp on a white glaze base it is still a Shorter made jug at the Crown Devon factory between 1964-1970.

SHORTER COPIES DANGER!

This is a very large minefield area for the collector and dealer alike. Being an ex-soldier I know about minefields. If its sign posted minefield keep out, you keep out, if it's not sign posted, and your not sure, don't go in, ask if it is safe. It's the same with Shorter Toby and Character Jugs. This book is your sign post, telling you where you can and cannot go in. Since Shorter's closure in 1964, then the move in with Crown Devon until 1970, many people have owned the Shorter moulds, so like the minefield we have to be careful where we tread. I know where 90% of the Shorter original moulds are, and I realise people have to make a living, but I have to say it wont be off our backs. I am totally against people producing jugs from the original Shorter moulds and selling them as originals, also you have the unscrupulous dealers buying these jugs and selling them as original jugs. To explain how unscrupulous they are, I have emailed people selling these copies as originals, to tell them they are selling copies as originals, their answer is we know, or mind your own business, so they are there to take people's hard earned dollars selling them as copies. Talking about copies, another practise of these copiers, is to buy Toby moulds from other firms, produce a jug from these moulds, and put a Shorter backstamp on them, knowing the Shorter name will sell better

than the original firm who made the mould. This folks is faking and deception, and its you the buyer that they are trying to deceive. You will see things on Ebay for instance 'Shorter Bob Hope for sale'. The Shorter experienced collector knows Shorter never made this jug, but if your new to collecting Shorter you will probably step into the minefield. Let's go back to the Shorter close-down that is the end of Shorter original jugs full stop. Then Crown Devon who took over Shorter, carry on making Shorter Jugs with Shorter moulds, they backstamp them with the Crown Devon stamp but still leave the Shorter name on them, they are from Shorter moulds but they are not Shorter made. Then Crown Devon close in the 1980s, the moulds go up for auction, quite a few people bought the moulds. Woods Potters of Burslem bought some of them. They produced a really nice copy, but did not hide the fact, they gave a certificate with the jug to say they had made them from Shorter original moulds. Nothing wrong with this they are very collectable items. Later Paul Singh from Staffordshire Fine Ceramics bought a lot of Shorter moulds and produced some really excellent jugs from Shorter moulds but renamed them and used his own backstamp. Paul still has these moulds but does not use them.. Now we are back to the present where we first started the minefield, this book will help you through the hazards, I have shown you all the original Shorter Toby and Character Jugs and their backstamps, and the reproduction and copy backstamps and put you on a safe path to a real collection of genuine Shorter jugs.

Sherwood copy backstamp

Common Shorter copy backstamp.

Copy of Woods Potters of Burslem backstamp.

Wood Potters of Burslem backstamp

Block Letters copy stamp.

Common Shorter copy backstamp.

Copy of original Shorter Backstamp.

SECTION ONE
SHORTER TOBY AND CHARACTER JUGS
1917-1970

BARNACLE BILL

What an amazing way to start a new book, a Shorter Character Jug which most people will never have heard of or seen before. This great find was previously unrecorded and discovered by Steve Mullins, co-author of *Toby and Character Jugs of the 20th Century and their Makers*. The jug was previously in a private collection for quite a number of years. The *Barnacle Bill* now resides in the Toby Museum in Illinois USA. The jug is unusual in that the model name on the base is hyphenated 'B-Bill'. The jug was nicknamed *Barnacle Bill* because of its sea-dog appearance, but what his original name was to be is any one's guess. The backstamp is the 'Genuine Staffordshire' mark and in raised letters 'B-Bill'.
Photography courtesy of Steve Mullins Collection.

Character Jug: 3¹/₄" Rating: At this time unique
Date: 1950s-1964

BARRISTER SERIES

We have given this character the name off the *Barrister* as his hair style is very similar to that of a barrister's wig. We also think it is much better if a Toby has the name of its character so that it can easily be recognised for reference. Originally, this set was probably issued as a tea service, of which we have the teapot, sugar bowl, preserve jar, milk jug, and the jug with a side handle. The milk or cream jug has been known as Toby No. 2 because of the '2' impressed on the base. This jug is also found in a single colourway version of either brown, blue, red or green, and also with 'Widecombe' inscribed on the front of the Toby. The same number '2' appears on the base of the small-sized *Coachman* jug. There is also a large 8" Toby in this series which was also issued in a single colourway of red, brown, blue, or green, what his duties are in the teaset is not known, maybe a hot water jug. The painted version illustrated shows what can happen when things go slightly wrong in the firing process. The paint has overheated and exploded over the front of the jug. The *Barrister* set has various backstamps, but more commonly it has the 'Genuine Staffordshire' mark.

Toby M/S: 8" Painted. Rating: Scarce. UK £60+ US $87+
Toby M/S: 8" All colours. UK £40+ US $58+
Toby S/S: 5" Painted and colours. UK £20+ US $29+
Character Jug: 4" Painted and colours. UK £15+ US $21+
Preserve Jar: 5" Rating: Scarce. UK £40+ US $58+
Preserve Jar: 4" Rating: Scarce. UK £40+ US $58+
Sugar Bowl: Two sizes. UK £20+ US $29+
Teapot: 6" Rating: Scarce. UK £60+ US $87+
Date: 1930s-1950

This teaset was produced by 'Staffordshire Fine Ceramics' in the 1980s from the original Shorter moulds.
Photography courtesy of Steve Mullins and David Fastenau.

BEEFEATER

This Toby Jug comes in three sizes and the Character Jug in two sizes and there is also a salt and pepper shaker which are quite rare. Other items in the *Beefeater* design that have just been recorded are a small pin dish and a wall mask. Also in the range are a table lamp (see page 63) and you may find a musical jug but as yet this is unrecorded. The wall mask has the 1920s backstamp 'Shorter & Sons, Stoke-on-Trent, England. The usual backstamp is 'Old Staffs Toby', but the more common is the 'Genuine Staffordshire' mark.

Photography for wall mask courtesy of Anne and Ken Jones. Collection. Photography for pin dish courtesy of Jan and Robin Cross collection.

Toby L/S: 8¹/₂" **Rating: Available. UK £50+ US $72+**
Toby M/S: 7¹/₄" **Rating: Available. UK £30+ US $43+**
Toby S/S: 4³/₄" **Rating: Available. UK £20+ US $29+**
Character Jug: 6¹/₂" **Rating: Scarce. UK £30+ US $43+**

Character Jug: 2" **Rating: Scarce. UK £25+ US $36+**
Salt Shaker: 2¹/₂" **Rating: Rare. UK £50+ US $72+**
Pepper Shaker: 2¹/₂" **Rating: Rare. UK £50+ US $72+**
Table lamp: 9" **Rating: Scarce. UK £50+ US $72+**
Pin Dish: 4¹/₂" x 4¹/₂" **Rating: Rare. UK £50+ US $72+**
Wall Mask: 4¹/₂" **Rating: Rare. UK £70+ US $101+**
Date: 1920s-1970

CAPTAIN AHAB

Captain Ahab is the famous character from a Herman Melville's novel, 'Moby Dick', 1851. It is amazing that nearly 100 years on Shorter decided to issue a Character Jug of this fictitious character, maybe it was to commemorate the 100 year anniversary of the famous novel. The *Captain Ahab* Character Jug is very well designed with the handle in the shape of a whaling ship in full sale. The backstamp is the 'Genuine Staffordshire' mark with the model name 'Captain Ahab' in raised lettering.

Character Jug: 4¹/₂" Rating: Scarce. UK £40+ US $58+
Date: 1950s-1964

CAT

An excellent animal type Toby from Shorter. The *Cat* is very similar to the small *Dog* Toby (page 22) in that it is the same size with a small variation in the pose. The backstamp is the 'Genuine Staffordshire' mark.
Photography courtesy of Jan and Robin Cross collection.

Toby Jug S/S: 5³/₄" Rating: Scarce. UK £40+ US $58+
Date: 1940s-1964

CAVALIER

The *Cavalier* was produced in a Toby Jug and a Character Jug. The Toby a very nicely modelled jug is seated with his sword in his right hand and down between his legs. The large M/S version shown is the honey glazed jug with the dark green backstamp, and in raised lettering the model name. I have not seen a *Cavalier* Toby Jug with the 'Genuine Staffordshire' backstamp in black ink. The Character Jugs handle is an extension of his long hair. The Character Jug shown has the 'Genuine Staffordshire' mark in black ink and in raised lettering the model name.

Toby Jug: 7" Rating: Scarce. UK £80+ US $116+
Character Jug: 4 $^{1}/_{4}$" Rating: Scarce. UK £40+ US $58+
Date: 1950s-1964

CHELSEA PENSIONER

This Toby comes in three sizes plus a small miniature Toby and recently found, a large-sized musical jug. The initials inscribed on the hat, stand for Royal Hospital. As with all the sets, the largest jug is the most sought after. There are two variations of the large jug, one version has the pensioner sitting on a base, the other version the pensioner's feet are level with the jug base. Until we have more information, the prices for both large jugs are the same. and why there were two different moulds used for the large *Chelsea Pensioner* is not known. The small Character Jug is quite difficult to find. Other items in this set are an ashtray and a cigarette box. The backstamps for the *Chelsea Pensioner* are 'Old Staffs Toby',

but more commonly it is the 'Genuine Staffordshire' mark. *Photography courtesy of Steve Mullins collection.*

Toby L/S: 9" Rating: Scarce. UK £130+ US $188+
Toby L/S: 8³/₄" Feet level with base. UK £130+ US $188+
Toby Musical Jug L/S: 8" Rating: Very Rare. UK £400+ US $580+
Toby M/S: 6¹/₂" Rating: Scarce. UK £50+ US $72+
Toby S/S: 4¹/₂" Rating: Available. UK £20+ US $30+
Toby Miniature: 2" Rating: Scarce. UK £30+ US $44+
Ashtray: 4¹/₄" x 3¹/₄" (see page 65) **Rating: Rare. UK £50+ US $72+**
Cigarette Box: 5" x 3¹/₄" Rating: Rare. UK £100+ US $145+
Date: 1930s-1964

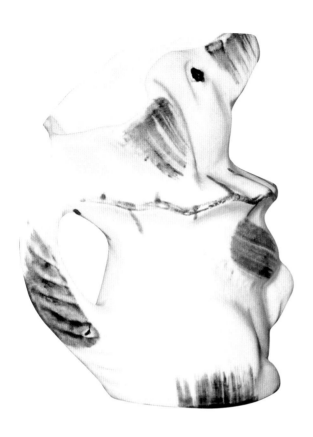

CIRCUS DOG

Not a great deal is known about this unusual item but that it was sent to me by a collector who describes it as a circus-type dog jug. I must apologise for the poor quality of the illustration, but it is better to show this than none at all. The backstamp is very unusual, in that it is impressed 'Shorter, England', but in black ink it reads, 'Purchased from, Dickens Old Curiosity Shop, London'. It will be interesting to see if any other items turn up with this backstamp.

Toby Jug: 4" Rating: Rare. Not seen for sale
Date: Not known

CLOWN

The *Clown* was issued as a single Character Jug but when it comes to buying this guy there is no clowning around he is a very rare jug. Backstamp for the *Clown* is the 'Genuine Staffordshire' mark.
Photography courtesy of Steve Mullins and David Fastenau.

Character Jug: 5" Rating: Very Rare. UK £200+ US $290+
Date: 1950s-1964

Coachman

The *Coachman* comes in four sizes, there is a Toby Jug and three Character Jugs. There is a very large Character Jug with just head and shoulders, a three-quarter size Character Jug which has more body, and a smaller head and shoulders Character Jug. There is also a large size green one colourway Character Jug. These, as with all early Shorter jugs, have a burgundy interior. The *Coachman* is backstamped mainly 'Old Staffs Toby', but is also found with the later 'Genuine Staffordshire' mark. I have yet to record one with a pre-1933 backstamp.
Photography courtesy of Steve Mullins and David Fastenau.

Toby Jug: 8" Rating: Rare. UK £100+ US $145+
Character Jug: 7¹/₂" Rating: Scarce. UK £60+ US $87+
Character Jug: Green: 7¹/₂" Rating: Scarce. UK £60+ US $87+
Character Jug: 6¹/₄" Rating: Scarce. UK £40+ US $58+
Character Jug: 4¹/₄" Rating: Scarce. UK £25+ US $36+
Date: 1920s-1950s

COCKEREL

Another excellent animal type Toby Jug from
Shorter. Again probably issued as a milk jug
but now in the Toby range. The backstamp is
the 'Genuine Staffordshire' mark.
*Photography courtesy of Jan and Robin Cross
collection.*

**Toby M/S: 6¹/₂" Rating: Rare. UK £40+ US $58+
Date: 1940s-1964**

COVENT GARDEN BILL

Covent Garden Bill comes in a pair, a large Toby Jug, and a Character
Jug. The jug is probably designed after one of the porters that worked
at Covent Garden fruit and vegetable market in London, The
character is seated on a basket with the handle in the design of a
banana and on his head is a basket which was used for carrying the
fruit to the market stalls. The market dates back to the 17th century,
and was used as a fruit and vegetable market until 1974. The
backstamp for this pair is the 'Genuine Staffordshire' mark.
Photography courtesy of Steve Mullins and David Fastenau.

**Toby L/S: 8" Rating: Rare. UK £150+ US $217+
Toby M/S: Reported, not verified.
Character Jug: 3¹/₂" Rating: Scarce. UK £40+ US $58+
Date: 1940-1950**

DICK TURPIN

The Dick Turpin Character Jug. Dick Turpin, being one of the more famous highwaymen immortalised in the history books was was hanged in York in April 1739. His fetters (ankle chains weighing 28lbs) are still on show in the York Museum. The handle of the Jug is a flintlock pistol, the main weapon of the highwayman. This is one of the six modern type jugs issued in the 1950s (see *Hayseed* page 30). The jug is backstamped with the 'Genuine Staffordshire' mark in dark green ink and impressed 'Dick Turpin'. We have shown these six jugs together, All are done in the honey-glaze finish as mentioned in the green backstamp paragraph (see page 9). The *Dick Turpin* is the top left hand jug in the photograph.
Photography courtesy of Steve Mullins and David Fastenau.

Character Jug: 5" Rating: Available. UK £30+ US $43+
Date: 1950s-1964

DOG, SMALL

The Small *Dog* is another animal type Toby which as you can see from the illustration is very similar to the *Cat* Toby (page 15), with only a slight variation in the pose and is well modelled with good detail. The backstamp is the 'Genuine Staffordshire' mark. *Photography courtesy of Jan and Robin Cross collection.*

**Toby S/S: 5³/₄" Rating: Scarce. UK £40+ US $58+
Date: 1940s-1964**

DICK WHITTINGTON

A small but quite hard to find Toby. Dick Whittington 1358-1423, had many stories written about him and is now immortalised forever. He was a merchant who later became the Lord Mayor of London. The jug was issued in various colourways, and is usually backstamped 'Genuine Staffordshire, Handpainted Shorter & Son Ltd, England'. Impressed 'Dick Whittington, S/S, Shorter, England'. I am also informed that a medium size *Dick Whittington* was issued but as yet there is no evidence to verify this.

**Toby S/S: 4¹/₂" Rating: Scarce: UK £70+ US $101+
Toby M/S: Reported not verified
Date: 1940s-1964**

Begging Dogs

This Staffordshire type dog, modelled in the begging position is, I am sure, from a Victorian mould, probably purchased by Shorter. These dogs have a handle, unlike the Staffordshire mantle dogs, which puts them into the Toby category. The Staffordshire mantle dogs went out of favour in the early part of the 20th century, but as you can see these are excellent jugs. I am pleased Shorter had the foresight to re-introduce them in the 1940s, my mantle piece would look rather bare without them. These dogs are well modelled, very lightly painted and have the grape design hat. The backstamp for this jug is 'Genuine Old Staffordshire, Shorter, England' in five lines and impressed with the number 737. Note the absence of '& Son Ltd' which is a very unusual backstamp. Jan and Robin Cross have Shorter Staffordshire figures with this backstamp and concurrent number 738 impressed without the '& Son Ltd' (see *Colonist* page 87). You will find modern copies of this Toby for sale which seem to be from the same mould but is is not known who makes them.

Toby Jug: Size: 9³/₄" Rating: Very Rare. UK £200+ US $290+
Date: 1940s-1950s

FATHER NEPTUNE

Father Neptune is a real gem of a Toby, a fitting tribute to the roman god of the sea. This design is so well modelled it smacks of a Betty Silvester style jug as in the D'Oyly Carte series (see pages 70-86). The *Father Neptune* is made in two sizes of Toby Jug and a Character Jug with the handle modelled as a sea-horse. There is also a table lamp, and a collector tells me there is also a musical jug in this design, which he once owned before selling it. Also illustrated above right is a medium-size *Father Neptune* commissioned from Staffordshire Fine Ceramics by Irene and Gordon Hopwood to celebrate the release of their book *The Shorter Connection*. As this is not an original Shorter jug, a price is not listed for this model. The backstamp for *Father Neptune* is the 'Genuine Staffordshire' mark, and in raised lettering, the model name and 'Shorter, England'.
Photography courtesy of Steve Mullins collection.

Toby L/S: 10" Rating: Rare. UK £150+ US $217+
Toby M/S: 7" Rating: Scarce. UK £70+ US $101+
Character Jug: 3³/₄" Rating: Available. UK £25+ US $36+
Table Lamp: 10" Rating: Scarce. UK £50+ US $72+
Date: 1950s-1970

FISH

Two superbly designed Toby Jugs of *Fish* by Shorter, again probably originally issued as water and milk jugs, now very sought after in the Toby range. The small, *Fish* shown above left, is backstamped with the 'Genuine Staffordshire' mark. The large *Fish*, shown right, also has the 'Genuine Staffordshire' mark but is impressed 'Shorter, England' with the number 36s.
Photography courtesy of Jan and Robin Cross collection.

Toby L/S: 9" Rating: Rare. UK £100+ US $135+
Toby S/S: 4¹/₄" Rating: Rare. UK £50+ US $72+
Date: 1940s-1964

FISHERMAN

A lovely well modelled jug, the *Fisherman* is one of my favourites. The detail is very clear and the paint work rather special. The Toby is 7" high and the Character Jug is 3³/₄" high and the handle for both is a fish, also the Toby has a brace of fish hanging from his left arm. There is also an ashtray with the *Fisherman* design and only just discovered is a medium size Toby Jug with a different hat which is round, without the lip or pourer and the fisherman's beard is black and grey, shown right of the illustration, which is the same as the Character Jug. The usual backstamp is the 'Genuine Staffordshire' mark, the model name and size and 'Shorter England' in raised lettering. Also Ashtray shown on page 65.

Toby M/S: 7" Rating: Scarce. UK £70+ US $101+
Character Jug S/S: 3³/₄" Rating: Available. UK £15+ US $22+
Ashtray: 4" x 3" Rating: Scarce: UK £40+ US $58
Date: 1940s-1950s

FLOWER SELLER

The *Flower Seller* is a very popular jug, not only with Shorter collectors, but also with those who collect seller series etc, and female Tobies. This very colourful jug was made in three sizes, sometimes thought in four, but the small 3" jug (shown far right), however, in our opinion and after long deliberation has been renamed *Hand Warmer* (see page 32). Our reason for doing this is that she does not have a basket of flowers in her hands but a muff or a hand warmer, the hat is a different style, the facial features are different, and the painting is completely different from the *Flower Seller*. The backstamp for the *Flower Seller* is either 'Old Staffs Toby', or the 'Genuine Staffordshire' mark.
Photography courtesy of Steve Mullins and David Fastenau.

Toby L/S: 9¹/₄" Rating: Scarce. UK £100+ US $145+
Toby M/S: 7" Rating: Scarce. UK £70+ US $101+
Toby S/S: 5¹/₄" UK £40+ US $58+
Date: 1930-1964

FRIAR TUCK

Friar Tuck was issued as a very large Character Jug, and seems to be paired with the large *Robin Hood* Character Jug. Both these characters are from the same legend of 'Robin Hood and his Merry Men'. The backstamp is the 'Genuine Staffordshire' mark.
Photography courtesy of Steve Mullins and David Fastenau.

**Character Jug: 7" Rating: Very Rare. UK £150+ US $217+
Date: 1950s-1964**

GARDENER

The *Gardener* is produced as a set of three toby jugs, but all the jugs are slightly different. The small size jug has a bird at his feet, the medium size jug has the bird on his knee and the large size jug has a tankard of beer in his left hand. This is a very fine set of Tobies which is more rare than the other sets. The backstamp is the 'Genuine Staffordshire' mark, and impressed 'Shorter England' with model name and size.
Photography courtesy of Steve Mullins and David Fastenau.

Toby L/S: 8^1/$_2$" Rating: Scarce. UK £135+ US $195+
Toby M/S: 6^3/$_4$" Rating: Scarce. UK £90+ US $135+
Toby S/S: 4^1/$_2$" Rating: Scarce. UK £40+ US $58+
Date: 1930s-1964

GROOM

The *Groom* is a Character Jug just recently discovered, which is rather strange because it is quite an early jug. The inside of the jug is burgundy which is only found on early jugs, but it has a post-1933 backstamp which reads 'Shorter & Son Ltd, Stoke-on-Trent, Made in Great Britain'. This jug, not having a name on the base as is the case with all Shorter's early models, was named by Anne and Ken Jones who are the owners of the jug.
Photography courtesy of Anne and Ken Jones collection.

Character Jug: 5¹/₄" Rating: Scarce.
UK £50+ US $72
Date: 1920s-1940s

GUARDSMAN

The *Guardsman* is a set of three toby jugs plus a small Character Jug. The handle of the small *Guardsman* Character Jug is a rifle which is on his left side. Also in this design is a salt and pepper shaker which is hard to find and an ashtray. To date, we have not found any evidence of a musical *Guardsman* as in the *Beefeater*, the *Sailor*, or *Scottie* sets, but it is very likely one was also made, we keep looking. The jug is usually backstamped with the 'Genuine Staffordshire' mark.
Photography above courtesy of Steve Mullins and David Fastenau. Salt and Pepper Shakers, photography courtesy of Jan and Robin Cross collection.

Toby L/S: 8¹/₂" **Rating: Rare. UK £130+ US $188+**
Toby M/S: 6¹/₂" **Rating: Scarce. UK £50+ US $72+**
Toby S/S: 4³/₄" **Rating: Available. UK £20+ US $29+**
Character Jug size: 2¹/₄" **Rating: Scarce. UK £30+ US $43+**
Salt Shaker: 2¹/₂" **Rating: Rare. UK £50+ US $72+**
Pepper Shaker: 2¹/₂" **Rating: Rare. UK £50+ US $72+**
Date: 1940s-1964

HAND WARMER

This Toby Jug has been re-named *Hand Warmer*. It was previously called the small *Flower Seller* (see page 27 for an explanation). We have followed the Victorian method of naming Tobies by their subject or by what they are doing, ie, *Snuff Taker*, *Hands in Pocket* Toby, etc. so the *Hand Warmer* is quite an apt name for this small Toby. The backstamp is 'Old Staffs Toby', or the 'Genuine Staffordshire' mark. On this Toby the stamp maker had trouble spelling, they missed the 'r' out of Shorter, so it reads 'Shoter'. It is not because the stamp has not taken, as is the case with some Shorter Tobies, it is very clearly a mistake which I expect Colly Shorter was not too pleased about. It is also impressed 'Shorter, England'.

Toby Jug: 3" Rating: Available. UK £20+ US $29+
Date: 1930s-1950s

HAYSEED

The *Hayseed* Character Jug, Hayseed being another word for a country bumpkin or yokel. The handle is in the design of a pipe. This is one of a series of six jugs issued in the 1950s (see page 21) from the Wilkinson factory with the honey-glaze finish. See green text backstamps for modern production painting. The jugs are of a modern production type as opposed to the all hand-painted earlier jugs, but they are a really good, well modelled jugs, more on the line of a Royal Doulton type Character Jug. The jugs are not impressed with the Shorter name, just backstamped with the 'Genuine Staffordshire' mark in dark green ink, and the model name impressed.
Photography courtesy of Steve Mullins and David Fastenau.

Character Jug: 5¹/₂" Rating: Available. UK £30+ US $43+
Date: 1950s-1964

HENRY VIII

A very decorative jug is *Henry VIII* sitting on his thrown, with really nice paintwork and lots of colour. Usual backstamp is the 'Genuine Staffordshire' mark. The small size jug is impressed 'King Henry VIII Shorter England'. The large jug is impressed 'Henry Eighth' or 'VIII Shorter England' and is a very rare jug. The small jug is not as rare as the large jug. You can find the smaller jug quite easy with the later green backstamp but alas it is not up to the quality of the earlier issue. The large jug can also be found with the later green backstamp, and even though the quality is not quite as good as the earlier large jug it is still a very rare jug. Bear this in mind if you are buying it.

Photography courtesy of Steve Mullins collection.

Toby L/S: 10" Rating: Very Rare. UK £200+ US $290+
Toby S/S: 5" Rating: Scarce. UK £50+ US $72+
Date: 1940s-1970

HIGHWAYMAN

The *Highwayman* Toby Jug is a very detailed and well modelled jug. There is a Character Jug and a very small Toby with a side handle, and an ashtray which has only recently been discovered. The Toby has a superb handle which is on a par with the D'Oyly Carte handles and is in the form of a black horse. This Toby is extra special in that it has the initials 'H S' one either side of the jug, low down near the base. The 'H S' are intertwined and painted on, so presumably Harry Steele the manager of Shorter 1932-1964 designed this jug. The Character Jug also has a good handle in the form of a flintlock pistol, the main weapon of the highwayman. The backstamp for these two jugs are the 'Genuine Staffordshire' mark, with the model name and size, plus 'Shorter, England' in raised letters. The small side-handled Toby has a mug of ale in its left hand, and is backstamped, 'Shorter & Son Ltd, Staffordshire, Made in England' in three lines.
Ashtray courtesy of Eddie Templeman collection.

Toby Jug: Size: 6" Rating: Rare. UK £70+ US $101+
Toby Jug: Size: 2" Rating: Scarce. UK £25+ US $36+
Character Jug: Size 3¹/₄" Rating: Rare. UK £40+ US $58+
Ashtray: 5" x 3¹/₄" Rating: Rare. UK £50+ US $72+
Date: 1940s-1964

Hollins

Called the Shorter *Hollins* Toby, and designed after the 1794-1820 original 'Ordinary Toby' produced by Hollins of Hanley, this jug is an excellent copy, as can be seen in Vic Schuler's book, *Collecting British Toby Jugs* where the original and the copy are illustrated together. This jug is modelled from the original Hollins 1790 mould purchased by Shorter. I fondly refer to this jug as the 'big fellow', for at 12" high they do not come much bigger. You will find him in various colourways, I have seen him with a red, a purple and a green coat. Notice the lightly painted face, which I refer to as the first period painting. Later versions have a more red face. This design is recorded as Shorter's first Toby in 1917, but as yet I have not seen one without 'Ltd' in the backstamp, dating those I have seen as post-1933. The usual backstamp is 'Old Staffs Toby' or the 'Genuine Staffordshire' mark and impressed 'Shorter England'. I think he is a must for any Shorter collection, being the essence of what Toby Jugs were all about in the 18th century, the famous Toby Fillpot.

Toby Jug: Size: 12" Rating: Scarce. UK £175+ US $253+ Date: 1917-1940

HUNTSMAN

The *Huntsman* is another Toby that is quite difficult to find. There is a Toby Jug at 7" and a Character Jug at 3³/₄" high. The jug has a dog by his side and is well modelled and has good detail. The handle on both items is a hunting horn. There are two versions of the large jug, one with the hat of a huntsman which is narrower and pours, ie as in a milk jug, the other version has a wide round hat without the pourer, shown left of illustration, the two obviously from different moulds. The backstamp is the 'Genuine Staffordshire' mark, with the model name and size and 'Shorter England' in raised lettering. We have only ever seen this jug in one colourway.

Toby M/S: 7" Rating: Scarce. UK £70+ US $101+
Character S/S: 3³/₄" Rating: Scarce. UK £30+ US $43+
Date: 1940s-1964

JOHN BULL

The British patriotic Toby Jug with his Union Jack shirt and the British bull dog by his side. The backstamp is the 'Genuine Staffordshire' mark. Be careful when trying to buy this fellow he is quite rare, and there are so many different later copies from the same mould. You will find him with a green backstamp, and without any markings on the base. The jug, shown left of the illustration is a modern copy, which has only just been discovered, which means that there was a larger *John Bull* mould made by Shorter, but as yet there is no evidence that it was ever released by Shorter. It is worth keeping a open mind as it would be a great find if an original turned up for sale.

Toby Jug: Size: 5" Rating: Rare. UK £50+ US $72+
Date: 1940s-1950s

JUDGE

The *Judge* is another very rare Shorter Toby, issued in a medium size. There is also a very striking teapot in this range and it has the words 'Justice' inscribed on the spout and 'Judge 42s' in raised lettering on the base. A different size model has been reported but not as yet verified. The backstamp is the 'Genuine Staffordshire' mark.

Photography courtesy of Steve Mullins collection.

Toby M/S: Size: 7" Rating: Very Rare UK £150+ US $217+
Toby S/S: Reported not verified
Teapot: 5" Rating: Very Rare. UK £150+ US $217+
Date: 1950s

KING AND QUEEN OF HEARTS

The *King* and *Queen of Hearts* are both small side handled
Tobies. I am almost sure *Queen of Hearts* is from the same
mould as the *Highwayman* but just painted differently. I have
not seen the *King of Hearts* as yet in any collection but it will
no doubt turn up. I have not handled this jug to see the
backstamp, but if it is from the same mould as the small
Highwayman it will be 'Shorter & Son Ltd, Staffordshire,
Made in England' in three lines, or the 'Genuine
Staffordshire' mark.
Photography courtesy of Steve Mullins and David Fastenau.

King of Hearts: Toby: Size: 2¹/₂" Not seen for sale
Queen of Hearts: Toby: Size: 2¹/₂" Rating: Scarce. UK £40+ US $58+
Date: 1940s-1950s

KOOKABURRA

The *Kookaburra* bird is, I think, an Australian kingfisher. This
jug was probably issued as a creamer or milk jug, but is now
collected in the Toby category. The painting is extra special and
is done in mottled colours making it a very striking jug. The
backstamp for the *Kookaburra* is, 'Shorter & Son Ltd, Stoke-on-
Trent, England' with the impressed number 304.
Photography courtesy of Jan and Robin Cross collection.

Toby M/S: Size: 6³/₄" Rating: Rare. UK £80+ US $116+
Date: 1930s-1950s

LONG JOHN SILVER

A beautiful jug is the Long John Silver, but I am not surprised as it was designed by Betty Silvester, and in my opinion a very underrated jug at present. You can see how closely it resembles the D'Oyly Carte issues, in fact it has the same handle as the *Pirate King*, which was designed by Betty. The sizes are also very similar to the D'Oyly Carte's being a large and small Toby issue. There is also a table lamp issued in this model, as shown left above. If you look closely under the handle by the base line you will see the name Silvester painted, but the name is not on all the jugs. Also in the S/S jug there is a blue shirt model of Long John as shown above right, which is a lot scarcer than the purple shirt model. The backstamp is the 'Genuine Staffordshire' mark, and is impressed 'Shorter England' with the model name.

Photography of Table Lamp and L/S, S/S Toby, courtesy of Steve Mullins and David Fastenau.

Toby Jug: L/S 10" Rating: Scarce. UK £80+ US $116+
Toby Jug: S/S 5" Rating: Available. UK £25+ US $36+
Toby Jug: S/S 5" Blue Shirt Variety. UK £50+ US $72+
Table lamp: 10" Rating: Scarce. UK £50+ US $72+
Date: 1940s-1964

LORD MAYOR

The *Lord Mayor* was issued as a medium size Toby, and also reported, but not verified, issued in a different size. This a well designed jug and quite hard to find. Just recently discovered is the *Lord Mayor* teapot which was not previously recorded. The backstamp is the 'Genuine Staffordshire' mark.
Teapot photography courtesy of Anne and Ken Jones collection.
Toby photography courtesy of Steve Mullins collection.

Toby: M/S 6¹/₂" Rating: Rare.
UK £150+ US $217+
Toby: S/S: Reported not verified.
Teapot: Size: 5" Rating: Rare.
UK £100+ US $145+
Date: 1950s-1964

MAC

Mac is a small Character Jug of a Scotsman. This is the first time *Mac* has been recorded, which is another of those Shorter mysteries. Why? The *Mac* is a 1950s-1964 jug, but as the *Mountaineer* (see page 45) etc, is very hard to find. This is one of the twelve jugs mentioned by Steve Mullins and David Fastenau in their book *Toby and Character Jugs of the 20th Century and Their Makers* as, referred to in the Shorter records, but not yet recorded. *Mac* has the 'Genuine Staffordshire' mark and in raised lettering on the base the model name. This *Mac* is the first one recorded and until more of these jugs are found it will have to be rated as very rare, and as such will carry a high price tag.
Photography courtesy of Anne and Ken Jones collection.

Character Jug: Rating: Very Rare
UK £150+ US $217+
Date: 1950s-1964

MARTHA

The name for this Toby might come as a surprise to Shorter collectors as it has always been known as *Mrs Farmer*. We thought the same until very recently, when out of the blue came a Toby Jug with the name on the base of *Mr Farmer*, which had always previously been known as *Nut Brown Ale* (see *Mr Farmer*). The now named *Martha* jug had always been paired with the previously named *Mr Farmer* jug which is now renamed the *Squire* (see page 61). Staffordshire Fine Ceramics, who now own the mould for this Toby, have issued it as *Martha*. The old *Mr* and *Mrs Farmer,* as we knew them, were one of the few Shorter Toby Jugs that were not named on the base. The Toby comes in two sizes and is backstamped 'Old Staffs Toby', or with the 'Genuine Staffordshire' mark. This latest information also raises the question of whether there was a *Mrs Farmer* Toby Jug issued by Shorter. At this moment, we have no evidence or knowledge of such a Toby Jug, but keep an open mind about it as you could be the one to find it. *Martha* Tobies in both sizes are very hard to find.
Photography courtesy of Steve Mullins collection.

Toby: L/S 7¹/₄" Rating: Very Rare. UK £150+ US $217+
Toby: S/S 4³/₄" Rating: Very Rare. UK £80+ US $116+
Date: 1930s-1950s

MIKE

In other reference books on Shorter this Toby has been called *Irish Mike*, where the name came from we do not know. The jug has just *Mike* on the base, so that is what we will call it. The jug is in the image of a country yokel type pig handler, who is seated on a pig with a violin under his right arm. There is also a Character Jug of *Mike*. The backstamp is the 'Genuine Staffordshire' mark.
Photography courtesy of Steve Mullins and David Fastenau.

Toby Jug: Size: 7¹/₂" Rating: Very Rare. UK £200+ US $290+
Character Jug: Size: 3³/₄" Rating: Very Rare. UK £100+ US $145+
Date: 1950-1964

MINIATURE TOBIES

The Shorter Miniature Tobies are very hard to list accurately as they are not named and are quite scarce and tend to be overlooked by a lot of collectors. I have listed the ones which I know of but there are more out there not yet recorded. They all have various backstamps.
Photography courtesy of Steve Mullins and David Fastenau.

Beefeater: Size: 2" (not illustrated, see listing page 14)
Chelsea Pensioner: Size: 2" (see listing page 17)
Guardsman: 2¹/₄" (not illustrated, see listing page 31)
Highwayman: 2¹/₄" (see listing page 34)
King and Queen Hearts: 2¹/₂" (not illustrated, see listing page 39)
Ordinary Toby: Size: 2" Three versions (two illustrated). UK £15+ US $22+
Soldier: Size: 2¹/₄" Rating: Scarce. UK £15+ US $22+
Dates: 1930s-1950s

MOUNTAINEER

The *Mountaineer* is a very rare Character Jug and at the moment this is the only version we have seen, or know of, which is owned by Steve Mullins and is in the Toby Jug Museum in Illinois, USA. We have received information about a medium size jug in this design, but as yet there is no evidence to verify this. The backstamp is the 'Genuine Staffordshire' mark.
Photography courtesy of Steve Mullins collection.

Character Jug: Size: 4¹/₂" Rating: Very Rare
UK £150+ US $217+
Character Jug: M/S reported. not verified
Date: 1940s-1964

Mr Farmer

Just recently two jugs have been found named *Mr Farmer* L/S on the base in raised lettering, the mould has also been altered to give the model a smaller pipe. The backstamp is the 'Genuine Staffordshire' mark in dark green ink, and the jugs are in the honey-glaze finish. This new information has led to the renaming of the former known *Mr* and *Mrs Farmer* (see the *Squire* and *Martha*). The early modelled Toby comes in two sizes and was also issued in a Rockingham style glaze. The earlier *Mr Farmer* model has the long pipe and is sitting on a barrel with the words 'Nut Brown Ale' on it. Usual backstamps are 'Old Staffs Toby', or the 'Genuine Staffordshire' mark. Why the later jugs have had the name 'Mr Farmer' added to the mould is not known at present. I might add that some of the long standing collectors think this jug looks more like a farmer than the former known *Mr Farme*r now re-named the *Squire*.
Photography courtesy of Steve Mullins and David Fastenau. Photography of later model courtesy of Eddie Templeman.

Toby L/S: 8" Later Model: Rating: Rare. UK £130+ US $188+
Toby M/S: 8" Early Model: Rating: Rare. UK £180+ US $261+
Toby M/S: 7¹/₄" Rockingham not seen for sale
Toby S/S: 4³/₄" Rating: Rare. UK £100+ US $145+
Date: 1920s-1970

MRS PUNCH

This *Mrs Punch* Toby Jug has been referred to as 'Judy' in other books but is named on the base as *Mrs Punch*. The 'Punch and Judy' as they are usually known as, go a long way back in our history books as theatre characters, but as a pair of Toby Jugs they are still very sought after by collectors. A recent copy of this jug from a Shorter *Mrs Punch* mould has just been sold for £31.00 (US $45.00) on Ebay Auctions. This copy is quite a good example and is well painted, we think it was made by Cortman Ltd, but still a very reasonable price as the original Shorter *Mrs Punch* Toby Jug is very rare and hard to find. The backstamp is the 'Genuine Staffordshire' mark and is impressed 'Mrs Punch, Shorter, England'.
Photography courtesy of Steve Mullins collection.

Toby M/S 6" Rating: Very Rare. UK £250+ US $362+
Date: 1940s-1950s

OLD BILL

Old Bill is a strange Character Mug which is classed as a Mug rather than a Jug and has a handle as a mug. He has the appearance of a squadron leader from the Second World War, with his large flowing moustache. The Mug was made in two sizes and is backstamped with the 'Genuine Staffordshire' mark, impressed 'Shorter England' with the number 667.
Photography courtesy of Steve Mullins and David Fastenau.

Character Mug M/S: 4" Rating: Scarce. UK £40+ US $58+
Character Mug S/S: 3¹/₂" Rating: Scarce. UK £30+ US $43+
Date: 1940s-1964

Old King Cole

Old King Cole design was issued in two sizes of Toby Jug, two sizes of teapot and a table lamp (see page 63). Recently recorded is a pin dish which is quite unusual as it is octagonal. Also a collector tells me he has a musical Toby Jug. The *Old King Cole* Toby Jug is very colourful with some slight variations in the painting of the crown. You will find jugs with a purple and yellow crown or a blue and yellow crown. The backstamp is the 'Genuine Staffordshire' mark and the model name impressed with 'Shorter, England'.
Photography of jugs courtesy of Steve Mullins and David Fastenau.
Photography of pin dish courtesy of Jan and Robin Cross collection.

Toby L/S: 10" Rating: Scarce. UK £100+ US $145+
Toby S/S: 5³/₄" Rating: Available. UK £30+ US $43+
Table lamp: 10" Rating: Scarce. UK £50+ US $72+
Toby: 10" Musical Jug: Rating: Rare. UK £400+ US $580+
Pin Dish: 3¹/₄" Rating: Rare. UK £50+ US $72+
Date: 1940s-1964

OUTRIDER

The *Outrider* Toby Jug is from the 'Queen's Men' series and he is the chap who rides on the Queen's coaches. This jug was issued in two Toby sizes. The backstamp is the 'Genuine Staffordshire' mark. The jug shown in the illustration is the small size *Outrider*.
Photography courtesy of Steve Mullins and David Fastenau.

Toby size: 7$^1/_4$" Rating: Very Rare. UK £200+ US $290+
Toby size: 4$^3/_4$" Rating: Very Rare. UK £130+ US $188+
Date: 1950s-1964

OWL

The *Owl* is one of Shorter's bird Tobies probably issued originally as a water and milk jug, but now collected in the Toby range. There is a good range of animal type Tobies to collect if that is your interest. The backstamp for the *Owl* is the genuine staffordshire mark.
Photography courtesy of Anne and Ken Jones collection.

Toby L/S: 8$^3/_4$" Not yet recorded.
Toby S/S: 5" Rating: Scarce. UK £40+ US $58+
Date: 1940s-1964

PARAKEET

Another of Shorter's bird Toby Jugs. A very lightly painted jug but with a nice effect. The *Parakeet* does not often come up for sale. This is another jug that is put down to the Wilkinson factory, but this version has the black ink 'Genuine Staffordshire' backstamp with the honeyglaze finish. It also is impressed Shorter England with the number 306. I have seen two other versions of the *Parakeet*, very Art Deco type jugs, but unfortunately I was unable to obtain an illustration of either model.

Toby Size: 9" Rating: Scarce. UK £100+ US $145+
Toby Size: 9" Art Deco: Rating: Rare.
UK £150+ US $217+
Date: 1930s-1964

PARSON JOHN

Parson John comes in two Toby sizes. The moulds for this jug were originally owned by Sampson Smith of Longton, and their jug was called 'Mr Pickwick', described in Vic Schuler's book, *Collecting British Toby Jugs*. *Parson John* is painted in what we call 'first period painting', and 'second period painting'. The first period 7" jug has a very pale face and hands and is a very lightly potted jug, weighing 0.340 kilo grams (shown right above). The second period 7" painted jug, which is a heavier potted jug, has a very red face and hands and weighs 0.465 kilo grams (shown left above). The difference 0.125 kilo grams which is the weight of a 3" Toby. There is also a variation in painting, the lightly potted jug he is leaning against a brown-coloured tree, and in the heavier potted jug he is leaning against a green-coloured tree. Backstamped 'Old Staffs Toby' or with the 'Genuine Staffordshire' mark.

Toby M/S: 7" Rating: Scarce. UK £50+ US $72+
Toby L/S: 8" Rating: Scarce. UK £80+ US $116+
Date: 1920s-1950s

PEDRO

The *Pedro* Character Jug is one of the six jugs produced in the late 1950s (see page 21). We are not sure who the *Pedro* character is but he is obviously a fisherman with the design of the handle in the form of a fish. The backstamp is the 'Genuine Staffordshire' mark in dark green ink, and is impressed 'Pedro'.
Photography courtesy of Steve Mullins and David Fastenau.

Character Jug: 5¹/₂" Rating: Available.
UK £30+ US $43+
Date: 1950s-1964

PEARLY KING AND PEARLY QUEEN

The *Pearly King* and *Pearly Queen* are a lovely pair of Toby Jugs and are quite rare. If you are wondering why the King has a banana handle and the Queen an eel handle, it is because these cockney characters were called costermongers, or costardmongers who sold fruit, vegetables, or fish, from a street or market stall, hence the banana handle for the King. The eel on the Queen's handle probably refers to jellied eels which is a delicacy of the cockney people. The backstamp for these jugs is the 'Genuine Staffordshire' mark. We have just received a report of two other sizes known in this model, but this has not yet been verified.
Photography courtesy of Steve Mullins collection.

Pearly King: L/S Not yet verified
Pearly King: M/S 7" Rating: Rare. UK £170+ US $246+
Pearly King: S/S Not yet verified
Pearly Queen: L/S Not yet verified
Pearly Queen: M/S 7¹/₂" Rating: Rare UK £170+ US $246+
Pearly Queen: S/S Not yet verified
Date: 1940s-1964

PIRATE

The *Pirate* Character Jug, is another
of the six modern type jugs issued
in the late 1950s (see page 21), with
the handle in the design of a parrot.
These six jugs are all very well
modelled. The backstamp is the
'Genuine Staffordshire' mark in dark
green ink, and impressed 'Pirate'.
*Photography courtesy of Steve Mullins
and David Fastenau.*

Character Jug: 4¹/₂" Rating: Available
UK £30+ US $43+
Date: 1950s-1964

POLICEMAN

The *Policeman* is modelled after the British policeman. There are three Toby Jugs in this
set, a large, a medium and a small size. The large 9" *Policeman* has just been listed on
Ebay Auctions which was previously unrecorded and has just sold for the amazing price
of US $855.00 (UK £586.00). This is the highest price ever paid for a Shorter Toby
excluding the D'Oyly Carte series. Naturally the rarity of this large jug was a
contributory factor to the amount paid and if a second jug were to emerge, it would
probably not reach such a high price. This jug is often referred to as 'PC 49', but is
actually impressed on the base 'PC 7'. The backstamp for this model is the 'Genuine
Staffordshire' mark, it is also impressed 'Shorter England' with the model size. It can also
be found with the 'Old Staffs' backstamp.
Photography courtesy of Steve Mullins collection.

Toby: L/S 9" Rating: Very Rare. UK £250+ US $362+
Toby M/S: 7" Rating: Rare. UK £140+ US $203+
Toby S/S: 5" Rating: Rare. UK £80+ US $116+
Date: 1940s-1964

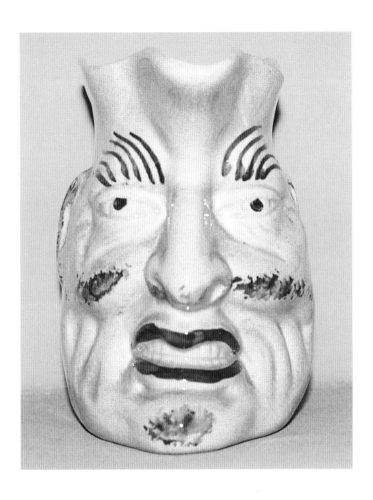

PUNCH

The large *Punch* Character Jug was yet another unrecorded jug which has just turned up for sale on Ebay Auctions. This *Punch* has a very menacing face, just the jug to put on the mantelpiece to keep the kids away from the fire. The jug is not named on the base, and has the backstamp that you usually see on the Shorter flatware and tea services. Maybe it was originally issued as a large water jug or pitcher. The backstamp is 'Shorter & Son Ltd, Stoke-on-Trent, Made in Great Britain', in blue ink.
Photography courtesy of Steve Mullins collection.

Character Jug: 6³/₄" Rating: Rare. UK £200+ US $290+
Date: 1930s-1950s

ROBERT BURNS

Robert Burns the famous Scottish poet and writer of traditional songs 1759-1796, was issued as a Character Jug by Shorter. Not much is known about this jug other than it was in the Lionel Bailey collection. We think it has since been sold on and at present we know of no-one else having this jug in their collection, therefore it must be classified as very rare. The backstamp is the 'Genuine Staffordshire' mark.
Photography courtesy of Steve Mullins and David Fastenau.

Character Jug: 4¹/₄" Rating: Very Rare. Not seen for sale
Date: 1950s-1964

ROBIN HOOD

Robin Hood was issued in two sizes, a Toby Jug and a very large Character Jug. Both jugs are very hard to find and do not often come on the market for sale. The Character Jug does not match the Toby in any way, but it does seem to be paired with the *Friar Tuck*, who was one of Robin Hood's Merry Men. The backstamp for both *Robin Hood* jugs is the 'Genuine Staffordshire' mark.
Photographs courtesy of Steve Mullins and David Fastenau.

Toby M/S: 7" Rating: Very Rare. UK £200+ US $290+
Character Jug: 8" Rating: Very Rare. UK £200+ US $290+
Date: 1950s-1964

ROYAL VOLUNTEER

The *Royal Volunteer,* is from the 'Queen's Men' series. The jug was issued in the medium size and the small size and is a very well designed jug. This jug is another of those hard to find Shorter jugs. The backstamp is the Genuine Staffordshire' mark.
Photography courtesy of Steve Mullins and David Fastenau.

Toby M/S: 7¹/₂" Rating: Very Rare. UK £200+ US $290+
Toby S/S: 4³/₄" Rating: Very Rare. UK £130+ US $188+
Date: 1950s-1964

SANTA CLAUS

This *Santa Claus* is by Crown Devon but is one of the jugs referred to in the Shorter records as mentioned in Irene and Gordon Hopwoods book *The Shorter Connection*. Steve Mullins and David Fastenau are sure this Crown Devon model is taken from an original Shorter mould and we would agree with them. We do not know of any collector who has an original *Santa Claus,* but if one does turn up it would be a very rare jug indeed. Therefore, as this is not an original Shorter jug, there is no price listed for this model.
Photography courtesy of Steve Mullins and David Fastenau.

SAILOR OR OLD SALT

This set of Tobies has two model names. H.M.S. Cheerio is just the name on the cap band which was usually the ship the sailor was serving on. The model names are *Old Salt* or *Sailor*. Which model name was used first I am not sure, but I think *Old Salt* at a guess. The surprise package of this set is the recent and marvellous find of a *Sailor* musical jug measuring 8" high, shown second from the left. Notice how much higher the base is to accommodate the musical mechanism. At this time this is the only one recorded. This then makes this a set of four Toby Jugs and a salt and pepper shaker. The backstamp is 'Old Staffs Toby', or the 'Genuine Staffordshire' mark, with 'Shorter England' impressed with the model name and size.
Photography courtesy of Eddie Templeman collection.

Toby L/S: 8¹/₂" Rating: Rare UK £135+ US $196+
Toby M/S: 6¹/₂" Rating: Scarce UK £80+ US $116+
Toby S/S: 4¹/₄" Rating: Scarce UK £40+ US $58+
Toby 8" Musical: Rating: Very Rare UK £400+ US $580+
Salt Shaker: 2¹/₂" Rating: Rare. UK £50+ US $72+
Pepper Shaker: 2¹/₂" Rating: Rare. UK £50+ US $72+
Date: 1930s-1970

SCOTTIE

The *Scottie* Toby Jug is one of a set. There are slight variations in the colourways, some of them are painted with a deeper red coat, there are also differences in the tartan. You may even find a *Scottie* with a plain red coat instead of a tartan one. There is also a large size musical jug as in the *Sailor* set and a table lamp (see page 63). It is also possible, as with other sets you may find a salt and pepper shaker, but as yet these are unrecorded. Only just recorded is a *Scottie* Wall Mask shown right. The backstamp for the *Scottie* is the 'Genuine Staffordshire' or 'Old Staffs Toby' mark, and impressed 'Shorter England', with the model name and size. There are also many with the later green backstamp.

Toby L/S: 8¹/₂" Rating: Available. UK £70+ US $101+
Toby M/S: 6³/₄" Rating: Available. UK £40+ US $58+
Toby S/S: 4¹/₄" Rating: Available. UK £25+ US $36+
Toby Musical Jug: Size 8" Rating: Very Rare. UK £400+ US $580+
Wall Mask: Size 4¹/₂" Rating: Rare. UK £70+ US $101+
Date: 1930s-1964

SHEIK

The *Sheik,* is modelled after an Arab Chieftain which is a more unusual subject for Shorter Character Jugs. This is one of the six modern type Character Jugs issued in the late 1950s (see page 21). The jug is backstamped with the 'Genuine Staffordshire' mark in dark green ink, and is impressed 'Sheik'.
Photography courtesy of Steve Mullins and David Fastenau.

Character Jug: 5¹/₂" Rating: Available. UK £30+ US $43+
Date: 1950s-1964

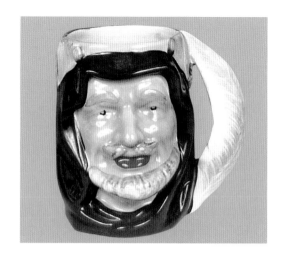

SINBAD

The *Sinbad* Character Jug, is another character from the book of legendary figures, also one of the six modern type Character Jugs issued in the late 1950s (see page 21). The jug is backstamped with the 'Genuine Staffordshire' mark in dark green ink and impressed 'Sinbad'. *Photography courtesy of Steve Mullins and David Fastenau.*

Character Jug: 4³/₄" Rating: Available. UK £30+ US $43+
Date: 1950s-1964

SOLDIER

The *Soldier* is one of Shorter's Miniature Tobies. From his attire it seems to be modelled on a First World War soldier, with his rifle on his right hand side. The Toby also has a side handle and you will find him in various colourways, red, blue and purple. The backstamp is 'Genuine Staffordshire, Made in England, Shorter & Son Ltd'.
Photography courtesy of Anne and Ken Jones collection.

Toby S/S: 2¹/₄" Rating: Scarce. UK £25+ US $36+
Date: 1930s-1950s

SMALL TOBY

This *Small Toby*, is another item thought to be originally a creamer, but is now collected as a Toby. You will find this jug in various colours and backstamped with the 'Genuine Staffordshire' mark and impressed 'Shorter England'.

Toby: 3¹/₄" Rating: Available.
UK £10+ US $15+
Date: 1930s-1950s

SOUTH AMERICAN JOE

South American Joe is an extremely well designed and painted jug which seems to have the Clarice Cliff or Betty Silvester touch about it. The Toby was issued in two sizes, with a recent find of a 10" wall pocket, as shown right. A medium size model has also been reported but not, as yet, verified. The backstamp is the 'Genuine Staffordshire' mark.
Photography courtesy of Steve Mullins collection.

Toby L/S: 10¹/₂" Rating: Rare. UK £150+ US $217+
Toby M/S: Reported not verified.
Toby S/S: 5¹/₂" Rating: Rare. UK £100+ US $145+
Wall Pocket: 10" Rating: Rare. UK £100+ US $145+
Date: 1950s-1964

SQUAT TOBY TEAPOTS

Toby Teapots usually come under the heading of Derivative Items, but some, such as the 'Squat Toby Teapot' have their own listing in the Toby section. The *Squat Toby Teapot* was produced in three sizes and is backstamped with the 'Genuine Staffordshire' mark. *Photography courtesy of Steve Mullins and David Fastenau.*

Teapot: 6" Rating: Available. UK £50+ US $72+
Teapot: 5" Rating: Available. UK £40+ US $58+
Teapot: 4" Rating: Available. UK £30+ US $43+
Date: 1930s-1950s

SQUIRE

The *Squire* Toby Jug is the renamed *Mr Farmer* (see page 46) which was renamed because of a recent discovery of a different Toby stamped 'Mr Farmer'. We think new name is very apt for this jug, as he has the look of a very stately looking 'squire' in a standing pose with his three-quarter length coat. The jug was produced in two sizes, and is backstamped 'Old Staffs Toby', or with the 'Genuine Staffordshire' mark. Tobies in both sizes are very hard to find.
Photography courtesy of Steve Mullins and David Fastenau.

Toby L/S: 7¹/₄" Rating: Very Rare. UK £150+ US $217+
Toby S/S: 4³/₄" Rating: Very Rare. UK £80+ US $116+
Date: 1930s-1950s

STANDING TOBY, SMALL

This small *Standing Toby* which we think was originally a creamer is now collected as a Toby in its own right. You will find it in various colours and is backstamped with the 'Genuine Staffordshire' mark and impressed 'Shorter'.

Toby: Size: 4" Rating: Available. UK £10+ US $15+
Date: 1930s-1950s

STANDING TOBY, LARGE

This is a real traditional style Toby, and is one of Shorter's early Tobies. Steve Mullins has this Toby in the Toby Museum in Illinois, USA. It has a burgundy interior, stands 11" high and comes in various colourways with a red, green or blue coat. The grape design painted on the hat varies with the different colourway. Being an early Toby he has the usual backstamp, 'Old Staffs Toby', but can also be found with the 'Genuine Staffordshire' backstamp.

Toby: Size: 11" Rating: Rare UK £180+ US $261
Date: 1920s-1950s

TABLE LAMPS

Although table lamps, are included with the entry for the Toby for the same model, we also show some here grouped together. Left to right, *Long John Silver, Old King Cole, Scottie* and *Beefeater*. As you can see the lamps are the same as the large size modelled jugs, the only difference being that they have tops added to take the light fitting. Recently recorded and not seen before is the *Daisy Bell* table lamp. The backstamp is the 'Genuine Staffordshire' mark. *Photography courtesy of Steve Mullins and David Fastenau.*

Beefeater: 9" Rating: Scarce. UK £50+ US $72+
Daisy Bell: (not illustrated): **10" Not seen for sale**
Father Neptune (not illustrated): **9" Rating: Scarce. UK £50+ US $72+**
Long John Silver: 9" Rating: Scarce. UK £50+ US $72+
Mother Goose (not illustrated): **10³/₄" Rating: Scarce. UK £50+ US $72+**
Old King Cole: 10" Rating: Scarce. UK £50+ US $72+
Pirate King (not illustrated): **10" Rating: Rare. UK £400+ US $580+**
Scottie: 9" Rating: Scarce. UK £50+ US $72+

TOBY

This Toby Jug, to me, is worth all the other Tobies in my collection. It is the 'Holy Grail' of Shorter Toby Jug collectors and is the only one I have found with a definite pre-1933 backstamp. This jug, shown on the left, is very simply decorated, with the eyes just two black dots. There is less detail than in the later Shorter jugs but he does have a separately moulded jug in his left hand, which is hollow. The base of the jug is completely glazed, not just the well as is usual, and the inside of the jug is maroon rather than a real red as in other early jugs. The backstamp is 'Shorter & Son, Stoke-on-Trent, England' with no impressed marks at all. The jug shown above centre is the 1950s issue which has a honey-glaze finish and the dark green backstamp and is impressed 'Shorter England' with the word 'Toby' S/S in raised lettering which was added to the backstamp sometime during the 1950s. The model name has been added later in the 1950s as is the same with the *Mr Farmer* model. The jug shown on the right is a 1930s issue backstamped 'Old Staffs Toby'.

Toby S/S: 5¹/₄" Rating: Scarce. UK £40+ US $58+
Toby S/S: Early Jug: UK £80+ US $116+
Toby S/S: 1930s Model: UK £60+ US $87+
Date: 1930s-1964

TOBY DERIVATIVES

Listed here are the ordinary *Toby* items illustrated top of page. The items with a specific design are not listed here but with their main entry in the Toby section, ie the *Fisherman* ashtray shown above left is listed on page 26. The ordinary *Toby* items are usually backstamped with the 'Genuine Staffordshire' mark.
Photographs courtesy of Steve Mullins and David Fastenau.

Toby plate: 10" Rating: Scarce. UK £25+ US $35+
Toby plate: 5" Rating: Scarce. UK £15+ US $22+
Toby cup: 2^1/$_4$" Rating: Scarce. UK £10+ US $15+
Toby cup: 3" Rating: Scarce. UK £10+ US $15+
Toby saucer: 4^3/$_4$" Rating: Scarce. UK £10+ US $15+
Toby sugar: 2^1/$_2$" Rating: Scarce. UK £15+ US $22+
Toby creamer: 3" Rating: Scarce. UK £15+ US $22+
Toby ashtray: 4^1/$_4$" x 3^1/$_4$" Rating: Scarce. UK £30+ US $43+
Toby cigarette box: 5" x 3^1/$_4$" Rating: Scarce. UK £50+ US $72+
Date: 1930s-1950s

TOWN CRIER

The *Town Crier* was probably first issued as a creamer for a tea or coffee service and has the number 435 impressed on the base, which is also found on sugar bowls etc. The toby-like figure on this jug has now been classed as a Toby and comes in four single colours, blue, brown and red, shown left and right of above illustration. The painted version, shown centre, can be found in various colourways with either a red, green or purple coat. The backstamps, on the single colour *Town Crier* are usually 'Shorter & Son Ltd, Stoke-on-Trent, England' or 'Made in Great Britain' and on the painted version impressed 'Shorter, England'. This little Toby is becoming harder to find and is often ignored on Ebay Auctions but to us he is a very important part of the Shorter collection.

Toby Size: 3³/₄" Rating: Scarce. UK £20+ US $29+
Price is for all colours
Date: 1930s-1950s

TOTEM POLE

The *Totem Pole* is one of Shorter's few advertising Character Mugs. The mug was issued for the promotion of Butlins holiday camps in the design of an American Indian totem pole face, with the handle designed as a tomahawk. The mug has the slogan 'Butlins Beachcomber Souvenir'. The backstamp is the 'Genuine Staffordshire' mark and is impressed with the number S912.
Photography courtesy of Steve Mullins and David Fastenau.

Character Mug: 4" Rating: Scarce. UK £30+ US $43+
Date: 1950s

TUDOR COURT

The *Tudor Court* Character Jug was made as a promotional piece for Tudor Court, Hobart, which is a tourist attraction in Tasmania. This is the only known painted version of the jug and is owned by Paul Singh of 'Staffordshire Fine Ceramics'. Why there are not more of these painted jugs we do not know. We have a single colourway version of this jug in blue, bought from Tasmania on Ebay, which we are almost certain is genuine and is backstamped 'Shorter & Son Ltd, Stoke-on-Trent, England' in green ink, which was the backstamp often used on tableware for Australia. We believe this piece was used at Tudor Court as a creamer or milk jug. The inscription on the jug is 'Hobart Tasmania Tudor Court'.
Photography of coloured jug, courtesy of Steve Mullins and David Fastenau.

**Painted Character Jug: 3¹/₂" Rating: Very Rare. Not seen for sale
Blue Character Jug: 3¹/₄" Rating: Rare. UK £150+ US $217+
Date: 1950s**

THE TRUMPETER

The *Trumpeter* Toby Jug is from the 'Queen's Men' series and is a very well designed and colourful jug. The jug was issued in two sizes, medium size and small size. We think the Queen's Men series would make an excellent collecting theme paired with the *Beefeater* series. The backstamp is the 'Genuine Staffordshire' mark.
Photography courtesy of Steve Mullins and David Fastenau.

**Toby size: 7¹/₄" Rating: Very Rare. UK £200+ US $290+
Toby size: 4³/₄" Rating: Very Rare. UK £130+ US $188+
Date: 1950s-1964**

UNCLE SAM

This American patriotic Toby Jug is very decorative and is an excellent tribute to a great nation. *Uncle Sam* who is dressed in a stars and stripes outfit has some lovely paintwork and the handle is modelled in the form of an eagle. The backstamp is the 'Genuine Staffordshire' mark, and impressed number 515. This *Uncle Sam* Toby Jug is very sought after by both British and American Toby collectors and also collectors of American patriotic items so you will experience very stiff competition on the website auctions. Since the terrible disaster of September 11th this Toby has doubled in value. *Photography courtesy of Steve Mullins and David Fastenau.*

Toby L/S: 8¹/₄" Rating: Rare. UK £180+ US $260+
Toby M/S: 5³/₄" Rating: Rare. UK £140+ US $203+
Toby S/S: 4¹/₄" Rating: Rare. UK £100+ US $145+
Date: 1940s-1950s

WINSTON CHURCHILL

The *Winston Churchill* Character Jug was issued in two sizes, one a large jug with an anchor and cable as a side handle, and a smaller jug which shows Winston smoking his favourite cigar. Both these jugs were issued in the honey-glaze finish with the dark green backstamp (see paragraph on green backstamps, page 9). As yet we have not seen either of these jugs with the 'Genuine Staffordshire' mark in black ink, only in dark green ink.
Photography courtesy of Steve Mullins and David Fastenau.

Character Jug: 6" Rating: Scarce. UK £80+ US $116+
Character Jug: 4¹/₂" Rating: Scarce. UK £40+ US $58+
Date: 1940s-1964

SECTION TWO

D'OYLY CARTE

The D'Oyly Carte issues are without doubt some of the best Toby Jugs ever produced by any pottery. Shorter went to great lengths to reproduce the costumes in every detail. Irene and Gordon Hopwood have covered this in their book the Shorter Connection, so I won't go over the same ground. The jugs were designed in the early 1940s, but owing to the Second World War were not issued until 1949. I was informed that to get the jugs ready to coincide with Colly Shorter and his wife Clarice Cliff's promotional trip to America, Canada, New Zealand, and Australia, the backstamp was handwritten on these early jugs, before the well known D'Oyly Carte scroll stamp was ready to use. The original issue was fourteen large jugs and fourteen small. After the Shorter closure, a few sets of the small jugs were issued in the early 1980s which are backstamped Rockingham, still later in the 1980s the new owners of the moulds, Sherwood China issued some sets of the small jugs but they were reduced in size, so were probably not from the master mould. Today they are still being produced as copies, but alas are very poorly done. The Gilbert and Sullivan opera's being such a popular theme with the opera collectors, it has the knock on effect of creating extra ordinary high prices for these jugs when they come on the market for sale. At the moment a

10" Poo Bah has fetched the highest price on Ebay auctions at $1,025.00, this sort of price will make this jug too expensive an item for the average collector. I have just been in touch with Mary Gilhooly who is the archivist for the D'Oyly Carte Opera Company. Mary has kindly checked through the D'oyly Carte archives to see if there were any documents relating to Shorter and D'oyly Carte on the subject of the Shorter D'oyly Carte Jugs, but alas and keeping with tradition on Shorter documentation there was nothing to be found in the archives.

If you are interested in the D'Oyly Carte Opera Company have a look at their web site it has a company history, plus the operas they perform today: http://www.doylycarte.org.uk

D'OYLY CARTE BACKSTAMPS

On the early issues of the jugs you will find them with the handwritten text. You will also find an ink stamp with the same text. The most common backstamp is the scroll stamp shown below centre. The other backstamp is the later reproduction backstamp by Sherwood. You will also see the ordinary Shorter copy backstamp on the D'oyly Carte Jugs.

Reproduced by
permission of the
D'Oyly Carte
Opera Co
Shorter & Son Ltd
Staffordshire
Made in England

Printed Backstamp

Original Shorter backstamp.

Sherwood reproduction backstamp.

BUTTERCUP

Buttercup is a character from the opera 'HMS Pinafore'. This jug is accredited as a Clarice Cliff design. There are two sizes of jug and an ashtray with the *Buttercup* design. To date, this is the only D'Oyly Carte jug which has not been seen for sale on Ebay Auctions. Whether or not this means they are more rare than the other jugs, remains to be seen. The usual backstamp is the Shorter Scroll mark, it can be found with the hand written backstamp, or without a backstamp, as usual caution is the word with the latter. Be sure the jug is the right size and is painted as the illustration.
Photography courtesy of Steve Mullins and David Fastenau.

Toby L/S: 10" Rating: Rare. UK £500+ US $725+
Toby S/S: 5" Rating: Rare. UK £300+ US $435+
Ash tray: 4¹/₄" x 3¹/₄" Rating: Rare. UK £300+ US $435+
Date: 1949-1964

DICK DEAD-EYE

Dick Dead-Eye is a character from the 'HMS Pinafore' opera. This jug was designed by Betty Silvester and the handle is modelled as a rope coming out from the rear of the hat and curled around a capstan (see page 85). The *Dick Dead-Eye* Toby Jug was made in two sizes and there is also a cigarette box with the same design. The usual backstamp is the Shorter Scroll, it can also be found with a hand written backstamp, or without a backstamp. Be careful if no backstamp, make sure the jug is the right size and is painted as the illustration above.

Photography courtesy of Steve Mullins and David Fastenau.

Toby L/S: 10" Rating: Rare. UK £500+ US $725+
Toby S/S: 5" Rating: Rare. UK £300+ US $435+
Cigarette Box: 5" x 3¹/₄" Rating: Rare. UK £300+ US $435+
Date: 1949-1964

DON ALHAMBRA

Don Alhambra is a character from the 'The Gondoliers' opera. The *Don Alhambra* Toby Jug was made in two sizes and designed by Betty Silvester. The usual backstamp is the Shorter Scroll, it can be found with the hand written backstamp, or without a backstamp. Be careful if it has no backstamp that it is not a copy, make sure that the jug is the right size and is painted as the illustration.
Photography courtesy of Steve Mullins and David Fastenau.

Toby L/S: 10" Rating: Rare. UK £500+ US $725+
Toby S/S: 5" Rating: Rare. UK £300+ US $435+
Date: 1949-1964

DUCHESS OF PLAZA TORO

The *Duchess of Plaza Toro* is a character from 'The Gondoliers' opera and the design for this jug is accredited to Clarice Cliff. The *Duchess of Plaza Toro* Toby Jug was made in two sizes and there is also an ash tray. The usual backstamp is the Shorter Scroll, it can also be found with a handwritten backstamp, or without a backstamp. Take care if no backstamp, copies were made, make sure the jug is the right size and is painted as the illustration. *Photography courtesy of Steve Mullins and David Fastenau.*

Toby L/S: 10" Rating: Rare. UK £500+ US $725+
Toby S/S: 5" Rating: Rare. UK £300+ US $435+
Ash tray: 4¹/₄" x 3¹/₄" Rating: Rare. UK £300+ US $435+
Date: 1949-1964

DUKE OF PLAZA TORO

The *Duke of Plaza Toro* is a character from 'The Gondoliers' opera. The design of this jug is accredited as a Clarice Cliff. There is also a cigarette box with the *Duke of Plaza Toro* design. The usual backstamp is the 'Shorter Scroll', it can be also be found with a handwritten backstamp, or without a backstamp. Take care if no backstamp, copies were made, make sure the jug is the right size and is painted as the illustration. *Photography courtesy of Steve Mullins and David Fastenau.*

Toby L/S: 10" Rating: Rare. UK £500+ US $725+
Toby S/S: 5" Rating: Rare. UK £300+ US $435+
Cigarette Box: 5" x 3¹/₄" Rating: Rare. UK £300 US $435+
Date: 1949-1964

JACK POINT

Jack Point is a character from 'The Yeoman of the Guard' opera. This design, made in two sizes and accredited to Clarice Cliff, is the only character from this opera to be used for a Toby Jug and has the handle in the design of a large axe (see page 85). The usual backstamp is the Shorter Scroll, it can also be found with a hand written backstamp, or without a backstamp. Take care if no backstamp, make sure the jug is the right size and is painted as the illustration. *Photography courtesy of Steve Mullins and David Fastenau.*

Toby L/S: 10" Rating: Rare. UK £500+ US $725+
Toby S/S: 5" Rating: Rare. UK £300+ US $435+
Date: 1949-1964

KATISHA

Katisha is a character from 'The Mikado' opera. This Toby Jug was made in two sizes with the design accredited to Clarice Cliff. There is also an ash tray in the *Katisha* design. The usual backstamp is the Shorter Scroll, it can also be found with a hand written backstamp, or without a backstamp. Take care if no backstamp, make sure the jug is the right size and is painted as the illustration.
Photography courtesy of Steve Mullins and David Fastenau.

Toby L/S: 10" Rating: Rare. UK £500+ US $725+
Toby S/S: 5" Rating: Rare. UK £300+ US $435+
Ash tray: 4¼" x 3¼" Rating: Rare. UK £300+ US $435+
Date: 1949-1964

KO-KO

Ko-Ko is a character from 'The Mikado' opera. The design for this Toby Jug is accredited to Clarice Cliff and was made in two sizes. The hair at the back of the head on the jug is curled in a ring to form a small handle. The usual backstamp is the Shorter Scroll, it can also be found with a hand written backstamp, or without a backstamp. Take care if no backstamp, make sure the jug is the right size and is painted as the illustration.

Toby L/S: 10" Rating: Rare. UK £500+ US $725+
Toby S/S: 5" Rating: Rare. UK £300+ US $435+
Date: 1949-1964

MAJOR GENERAL

The *Major General* is a character from 'The Pirates of Penzance' opera. This jug was made in two sizes has been accredited as a Clarice Cliff design with the handle is designed as part of a castle wall (see page 85). The usual backstamp is the Shorter Scroll, or can be found with a hand written backstamp. also found without a backstamp. Take care if no backstamp, make sure the jug is the right size and is painted as the illustration.
Photography courtesy of Steve Mullins and David Fastenau.

Toby L/S: 10" Rating: Rare. UK £500+ US $725+
Toby S/S: 5" Rating: Rare. UK £300+ US $435+
Date: 1949-1964

MIKADO

Mikado is the main character from 'The Mikado' opera. This Toby Jug was made in two sizes and is accredited as a Clarice Cliff design. There is also a cigarette box in the *Mikado* design. The usual backstamp is the Shorter Scroll, and it can also be found with a handwritten backstamp, or without a backstamp. Take care if no backstamp, copies were made, make sure the jug is the right size and is painted as the illustration. *Photography courtesy of Steve Mullins and David Fastenau.*

Toby L/S: 10" Rating: Rare. UK £500+ US $725+
Toby S/S: 5" Rating: Rare. UK £300+ US $435+
Cigarette Box: 5" x 3 ¼" Rating: Rare. UK £300+ US $435+
Date: 1949-1964

PIRATE KING

The *Pirate King* is a character from 'The Pirates of Penzance' opera. This Toby Jug was made in two sizes along with a cigarette box, and a table lamp and was designed by Betty Silvester. The handle is modelled as a skull and crossed bones (see page 85) which was also used on the *Long John Silver* Toby Jug, also designed by Betty Silvester. We have information from a collector that he has a musical jug with the *Pirate King* design which makes this the only musical jug in any design recorded for the D'Oyly Carte issue. The Toby Jug has the usual Shorter Scroll backstamp, but can also be found with a hand written backstamp, or without a backstamp Take care if no backstamp, make sure the jug is the right size and is painted as the illustration. *Photography courtesy of Steve Mullins and David Fastenau.*

Toby L/S: 10" Rating: Rare. UK £500+ US $725+
Toby S/S: 5" Rating: Rare. UK £300+ US $430+
Cigarette Box: 5" x 3¹/₄" Rating: Rare. UK £300+ US $430+
Table Lamp: 10" Rating: Rare. UK £400+ US $580+
Toby: 10" Musical Jug: Rating: Very Rare. UK £500+ US $725+
Date: 1949-1964

PIRATE MAID

The *Pirate Maid* is a character from 'The Pirates of Penzance' opera. The *Pirate Maid* Toby Jug was designed by Betty Silvester and was made in two sizes but does not have a conventional type handle, as her left arm modelled as the handle. There is also an ashtray with the *Pirate Maid* design. The Toby Jug has the usual Shorter Scroll backstamp, but can also be found with a hand written backstamp, or without a backstamp Take care if no backstamp, make sure the jug is the right size and is painted as the illustration.

Toby L/S: 10" Rating: Rare. UK £500+ US $725+
Toby S/S: 5" Rating: Rare. UK £300+ US $435+
Ash tray: 4^1/$_4$" x 3^1/$_4$" Rating: Rare. UK £300+ US $435+
Date: 1949-1964

POOH BAH

Pooh Bah is a character from 'The Mikado' opera. The *Pooh Bah* design, accredited to Clarice Cliff was made in two sizes of Toby Jug with the handle modelled as a bunch of keys, and an cigarette box. To date this Toby Jug is the most expensive recorded at $1,025 (UK £706) on Ebay Auctions, a very sought after item. The usual backstamp is the Shorter Scroll, it can also be found with a handwritten backstamp, or without a backstamp. Take care if no backstamp, make sure it is not a copy and that the jug is the right size and is painted as the illustration. *Photography courtesy of Steve Mullins and David Fastenau.*

Toby L/S: 10" Rating: Rare. UK £600+ US $850+
Toby S/S: 5" Rating: Rare. UK £300+ US $435+
Cigarette Box: 5" x 3¹/₄" Rating: Rare. UK £300+ US $430+
Date: 1949-1964

SIR JOSEPH PORTER

Sir Joseph Porter is a character from the 'HMS Pinafore' opera. The *Sir Joseph Porter* design, accredited to Clarice Cliff, was made in two sizes with the handle modelled as a ships helm (see page 85). The Toby Jug has the usual Shorter Scroll backstamp, but can also be found with a hand written backstamp, or without a backstamp Take care if no backstamp, make sure the jug is the right size and is painted as the illustration.
Photography courtesy of Steve Mullins and David Fastenau.

Toby L/S: 10" Rating: Rare. UK £500+ US $725+
Toby S/S: 5" Rating: Rare. UK £300+ US $435+
Date: 1949-1964

D'OYLY CARTE

HANDLES AND REPRODUCTIONS

Here are some of the extremely well designed handles of the D'Oyly Carte series Toby Jugs. Shown left to right, *Major General, Pirate King, Dick Dead-Eye, Sir Joseph Porter*, and *Jack Point*.

Illustrated here are some of the later reproductions, 1980s, probably produced by Sherwood, of the small-sized Toby Jugs which are shown to the right of its Shorter original. Note how much smaller they are than the original. Illustrated left to right, *Pirate Maid, Ko- Ko*, and *Mikado*. These reproductions are of quite good quality, and for those who cannot afford the original Shorter Toby Jugs, too expensive for most of us, are very affordable at, £30-£40 ($43-$58) and would make a good addition to your collection. The D'Oyly Carte copies that are being reproduced today from Stoke-on-Trent are badly made and are generally of poor quality, even though they are from the Shorter original moulds. *Photography courtesy of Steve Mullins and David Fastenau.*

SECTION THREE

STAFFORDSHIRE ITEMS

We thought a nice way of closing the book would be to show you some other Shorter Staffordshire items available for you to collect. Having said this, these items seem to be quite rare. We have only seen one pair of Staffordshire mantle dogs for sale on Ebay Auctions. As *Daisy Bell* and *Mother Goose* were designed as Spill Vases we have taken them out of Toby Jug category, and included them in this section. If you have any other items of Staffordshire pottery not shown in this, or other sections of this book, however slight the variation, i.e. size, colour etc, please let us know about them with as much detail, preferably a photograph, if possible. We have not included a price guide in this section with the exception of *Daisy Bell* and *Mother Goose*, as not enough is known about the Staffordshire issues, but we do know that their absence from the market makes them rare and very expensive items.

COLONIST FIGURES

A very unusual pair of colonist figures seated on a high back bench. Jan and Robin tell me they bought these items in America while on holiday. They went into an antique shop just on the off-chance, the way you do, full of expectation of that good find. Asked the owner if he have any Shorter items, he produced these colonist figures. Jan could hardly contain herself, you know the feeling folks you just want to shout! yippee ! Jan and Robin think they were made for the American market. The backstamp is 'Genuine, Old, Staffordshire, Shorter, England. with the impressed number 738, Note: this is the con-current number on from the *Begging Dog* (see page 23).
Photography courtesy of Jan and Robin Cross collection.

Colonist Figures: 5" Rating: Rare. Not seen for sale.
Date: 1940s-1950s

DAISY BELL SPILL VASE

This *Daisy Bell* is not a Toby, but is a Spill Vase which was designed for the mantlepiece to hold the spills or tapers for lighting cigars or the gaslights etc. The *Daisy Bell* was issued in two sizes, plus a wall pocket, and a 10" plate the Daisy Bell is another of the extremely well designed jugs by Betty Silvester, it has her inscribed name around the wheel of the bike. One of our collecting friends thinks this vase was designed in the likeness of Clarice and Colly Shorter, but there is no evidence to support this (a nice thought Darrell). The backstamp for this vase is the 'Genuine Staffordshire' mark.
Photography courtesy of Steve Mullins and David Fastenau.

Daisy Bell: L/S 10" Rating: Scarce. UK £70+ US $101+
Daisy Bell: S/S 5" Rating: Available. UK £30+ US $43+
Wall Pocket. Rating: Rare. Not seen for sale
Plate: 10" Rating: Rare. Not seen for sale
Date: 1940s-1964

STAFFORDSHIRE DOGS, LARGE

A truly exceptional pair of traditional Staffordshire Dogs. It has occurred to me that Shorter might have purchased moulds for these traditional Staffordshire Dogs from other companies that had gone out of business and are probably the original early Victorian moulds which dropped from favour at the turn of the 19th century. As with the medium-sized Staffordshire Dogs shown, Shorter tried with the painting, to capture the essence of a male and a female dog. The dog shown on the left, is slightly larger with more whiskers than the probable female on the right. Notice also the similar painting as the *Begging Dogs,* page 23, shown in Toby Jug section. The backstamps for the dogs is the 'Genuine Staffordshire' mark.
Photography courtesy of Anne and Ken Jones collection.

Dogs L/S: 9¹/₂" Rating: Rare. Not seen for sale
Date: 1940s-1950s

STAFFORDSHIRE DOGS, MEDIUM

What a pair of show stoppers! We think you would have to wait a long time to see a nicer pair of Staffordshire Dogs than these. Besides their superb painting, what is extra special is they are obviously male and female dogs. The dog on the left of the illustration is the male as he is slightly taller and has whiskers on a very broad snout, the female, on the right, has a more petite snout and no whiskers. The backstamp is the 'Genuine Staffordshire' mark and impressed with the number 611.
Photography courtesy of Jan and Robin Cross.

Dogs M/S: 7³/₄" Rating: Rare. Not seen for sale.
Date. 1940s-1950

STAFFORDSHIRE DOGS, SMALL

A small pair of Staffordshire mantle dogs. We think these dogs are dalmations, but they only have a few spots on them. Notice that they are both looking the same way. The backstamp for the dogs is the 'Genuine Staffordshire' mark. *Photography courtesy of Jan and Robin Cross collection.*

Dogs S/S: 5" Rating: Rare. Not seen for sale
Date: 1940s-1950s

DRUMMER BOY

The *Drummer Boy* a really lovely Staffordshire figure. He has his own base, but is also mounted on a further base. This figure is one of those Shorter items that could quite easily be missed as he only has the Shorter export backstamp 'Made in Great Britain, but has the impressed number 439. *Photography courtesy of Jan and Robin Cross collection.*

Drummer Boy: 6" Rating: Rare. Not seen for sale
Date: 1930s-1940s

FRUIT SELLER

A superb pair of Staffordshire figures. Jan and Robin have named these guys the *Fruit Seller*. Both figures shown are the same model but with a variation in the painting. *The Fruit Seller* is seated with a basket of fruit in his left arm, and is holding an apple in his right hand. The backstamp is the 'Old Staffs toby mark.
Photography courtesy of Jan and Robin Cross collection.

Fruit seller: 6" Rating: Rare
Not seen for sale
Date: 1930s-1940s

GARDENER

These were the first Staffordshire figures we saw from the Shorter issues, and we were very impressed with them. The pair illustrated are the same model but with a variation in the painting. The figure is not named on the base but as you can see he is leaning on a spade, and in his right arm is a plant-pot full of flowers, so we have named him the *Gardener*. The backstamp is the 'Old Staffs' Toby mark.
Photography courtesy of Jan and Robin Cross collection.

Gardener figure: 6" Rating: Rare. Not seen for sale
Date: 1930s-1940s

MOTHER GOOSE

The *Mother Goose* design Spill Vase as is the *Daisy Bell*, (see page 88), both are finely modelled and well painted. *Mother Goose* was issued in two sizes of vase plus a wall pocket and a table lamp. As yet we have no evidence of a plate being issued in this design as with the *Daisy Bell*. The backstamp is the 'Genuine Staffordshire' mark.

Photography courtesy of Steve Mullins collection.

Spill Vase: 10³/₄" Rating: Scarce. UK £110+ US $160+
Spill Vase: 5¹/₄" Rating: Scarce. UK £40+ US $58+
Wall Pocket: 10³/₄" Rating: Rare. Not seen for sale
Table Lamp: 10³/₄" Rating: Rare. Not seen for sale
Date: 1940s-1950s

SHEEP

Another lovely Staffordshire item from Shorter. The *Sheep* Spill Vases, we imagine, but are not certain, were issued as a pair, one for each side of the mantlepiece. Each are modelled with slight differences, the figure shown on the left is slightly larger and has the impressed number 605, the smaller version shown on the right has the impressed number 606. The backstamp is the same for both models 'Genuine Old Staffordshire Shorter England' in five lines.
Photography courtesy of Jan and Robin Cross collection.

Sheep: 5" Rating: Rare
UK £60+ US $90+
Sheep: 4³/₄" Rating: Rare
UK £60+ US $90+
Date: 1940s-1950s

WHISKEY FLASK

This is a very unusual Shorter item, and for want of a better description we are calling this a Whiskey Flask. If anyone does know what it was issued for, please email me as we would love to know. We are not sure if this should have had a ceramic tapered stopper, or if it was issued with a cork stopper. Shown in blue, we think it has the look of *Winston Churchill* about it. The backstamp is the unusual light green ink, 'Shorter & Son Ltd, Stoke-on-Trent, England'. Also, in raised lettering, 'Made in England'. We have seen this backstamp on items exported to Australia.
Photography courtesy of Anne and Ken Jones collection.

Whiskey flask: 8¹/₄" Rating: Rare. Not seen for sale
Date: 1940s-1950s

INDEX